For those seeking to pray with purpose and focus on what matters most.

Copyright

Prayers of Eternal Significance: A Prayer Reset for What Matters Most – Align Your Prayer Life with God's Will, by Stephen H Berkey, published by Get Wisdom Publishing, Box 465, Thompsons Station, TN 37179,

Printed in the United States of America.

ISBN 978-1-952359-83-5 (paperback)
ISBN 978-1-952359-84-2 (ebook)
Audiobook available (Amazon.com and audible.com)

For more information about Get Wisdom Publishing:

https://getwisdompublishing.com/

The Wisdom Prayer Series

Prayers of Eternal Significance

A Prayer Reset for What Matters Most
Align Your Prayer Life with God's Will

Stephen H Berkey

Contents

Part 3 - Prayers For the World

PART 4 — PRAYERS FOR YOUR LIFE

Introduction

Most Christians pray. They ask for help protection, provision, or relief. They pray when life is uncertain and when something needs to change. Their prayer is familiar, natural, and sincere. But there is a question most believers never stop to consider: **Am I praying for what matters most?**

You can pray often and sincerely and still be misaligned. You can be consistent in prayer and still be focused on what is temporary. Often, prayers are centered on immediate needs and changing circumstances. The problem is that what has eternal significance receives much less attention.

What you consistently pray for shapes the direction of your life.

If your prayers are centered on comfort and outcomes, your life will gradually follow those priorities. If your prayers are centered on spiritual alignment, transformation, and what endures, your life will begin to reflect those priorities instead.

WHY A PRAYER RESET IS NECESSARY

Prayer does not usually collapse; it drifts. Not because of poor intent, but because of subtle shifts in focus. Life becomes full and pressures just naturally increase. Responsibilities multiply and over time, prayer becomes reactive instead of intentional.

You begin to pray about what is urgent instead of about what is essential. You begin to pray for relief instead of transformation. You pray for specific outcomes instead of spiritual alignment.

None of these are wrong, but they are incomplete. Without spiritual alignment, prayer becomes centered on what is current or temporary. When prayer is misaligned, life follows that same direction. This is why a reset is often necessary.

A reset does not replace prayer – it realigns it.

OUR MODEL: HOW JESUS AND PAUL PRAYED

When you look carefully at the prayers recorded in Scripture, a pattern emerges. Jesus did not generally pray for ease, comfort, or immediate outcomes. He prayed for alignment with the Father's will, for endurance under pressure, for unity, and for faithfulness in what mattered most. Paul prayed the same way. He consistently prayed for things like:

- Spiritual understanding and wisdom
- Strength and endurance under pressure
- Growth in love, faith, and character
- Alignment with truth and purpose
- Lives that produced lasting fruit

These are eternally significant prayers. They are not focused on worldly conditions. Rather, they are centered on lasting transformation. This book is built on that same pattern.

WHAT THIS BOOK WILL DO FOR YOU

This book is about what to pray for if you want your life to change in the ways that matter most. Each chapter focuses on a subject of eternal significance: areas that shape your character, your decisions, your relationships, and your long-term impact. As you move through this book, you will:

- Clarify what truly matters
- Recognize where your current prayers are incomplete
- Identify specific patterns that are limiting your growth
- Learn how to redirect your prayers with purpose
- Be encouraged to take practical steps that produce real change

This journey is not theoretical or something to be considered for possible future attention.

It is for you to use immediately.

How to Use This Book

This is a book to use deliberately and slowly. Allow each subject to resonate in your heart. Each chapter is designed to help you identify where your prayers may be misaligned and then correct them with clarity and purpose.

The value of this book is in letting it reshape how you pray. Each chapter follows a similar process:

- ***Reframe the priority*** – changing how you think about the subject
- ***Define what it means*** – making it clear and practical
- ***Expose the gap*** – identifying if misalignment exists
- ***Pray differently*** – showing you how you can pray more effectively
- ***Examine your life*** – illustrating how it looks oriented with an eternal perspective

Do not rush this process. Take one subject at a time. Read it carefully. Answer the questions honestly and consider the implications. Pray deliberately and act specifically.

There are several different ways to use this book:

1. A 34-Day Prayer Reset
Read one chapter daily. Move slowly through the book. Each day read the chapter. Pray the transformational prayer. Engage the suggested practical step. This will create a full reset of your prayer life over five weeks. Do not rush.

2. Focused Growth by Category
Work through one of the four Parts at a time—God, others, the world, or your own life. This allows you to correct specific known imbalances you discover in your prayer life.

3. Diagnostic Use
Start where you already know there is a gap or weakness. If you rarely pray for others, begin in Part 2. If your prayers are mostly centered on immediate needs, begin in Part 1.

4. Ongoing Reference
Return to chapters as needed. They are meant to help bring your prayers back into alignment whenever drift occurs.

WHAT YOU SHOULD EXPECT

This book is intentionally direct. At times, it may feel uncomfortable. You may recognize patterns you have not noticed before. You may see that some of your prayers have been incomplete, reactive, or misdirected.

This is meant to help and encourage you. Clarity and understanding come before improvement. And correction must occur before meaningful change. You will not be asked to *do* more. You will be asked to *focus differently.*

BEFORE YOU BEGIN

Do not approach this book as a collection of prayers. Again, approach it as a reset. We are not suggesting you need to improve your normal prayer language. We are focused on aligning your priorities and will concentrate on what truly matters. You may not need to make wholesale changes to your prayer time, but you likely need to make a conscious change on the nature of your prayers.

These steps will establish direction. And, direction shapes your life. If you are willing to examine your current patterns, adjust what is misaligned, and act on what becomes clear, this book will help you change the direction of your prayer and your life.

Choose a starting point and begin! If you let your prayers change, your life will follow.

Common Ways We Drift in Prayer

Most people do not intentionally misalign their prayers. It happens gradually. Watch for these patterns:

- **Praying only for immediate needs**
  Your prayers are always focused on problems, pressures, and personal concerns.

- **Avoiding prayers that require change**
  You ask for help, but not for transformation.

- **Focusing on outcomes, not alignment**
  You want God to act, but do not ask how you should respond or change.

- **Neglecting others and the broader mission**
  Your prayers rarely move beyond your own life.

- **Repeating familiar prayers without examination**
  You pray what you have always prayed without questioning if it is still appropriate.

- **Substituting activity for alignment**
  You pray regularly, but not thoughtfully.

- **Ignoring what your prayers reveal**
  You never stop to ask what your requests say about your priorities.

Left uncorrected, these patterns will shape your life in subtle but powerful ways. A reset begins by recognizing them.

Reset your prayers and improve your life.

PART 1 – PRAYERS FOR GOD

Realigning Your Heart with God

This section has one purpose: to move God back to the center of your prayers and your life.

You can pray regularly and still remain centered on yourself. You can speak to God, ask for help, and seek direction while your priorities, desires, and focus remain unchanged. When your prayer begins with God, who He is, what He desires, and what He is doing, your life will change.

If your prayers are not centered on God, they will drift. When prayer drifts, life follows. What you consistently bring before God reveals what you believe matters most.

Remember, God is the center of your life.

Begin here and return often. If you move away from God, everything will slowly shift back to self.

Chapter 1
LOVING GOD FULLY

Prayers of Eternal Significance – Wholehearted Devotion

1. REFRAME THE PRIORITY

We pray for help and provision on a regular basis. But how often do we pray to love God more? Jesus called this the greatest commandment. It is not one priority among many, but the foundation of all others.

If love for God is weak, everything else becomes misaligned. Obedience will feel burdensome and worship will become routine. Our prayer time will turn into a list of requests rather than a relationship.

A prayer life centered on eternal significance begins here, not with what we need from God, but with how we love Him.

2. WHAT THIS LOOKS LIKE

Loving God fully begins with the condition of your heart and the pattern of your life. To love God is to:

- Desire Him above competing interests
- Seek Him regularly and intentionally
- Trust Him when outcomes are uncertain
- Obey Him when it is difficult
- Delight in both His presence and provision
- Remain loyal when following Him costs something

3. EXPOSE THE GAP

Most believers say they love God, but live with divided loyalties. The real question is this: What competes with Him? The competition is usually quiet and often subtle:

- comfort competing with surrender
- control competing with trust
- approval competing with devotion
- busyness crowding out pursuit

You are not lacking love. You are dividing it. We rarely walk away from God. We simply drift, one neglected moment at a time. We speak of love, but live with divided attention. Until this gap is recognized, it will not be addressed.

4. HOW TO PRAY DIFFERENTLY

When love for God is not central, your prayers reflect it. You will pray for relief, solutions, direction, or provision. These are not wrong, but they are incomplete. Rarely do you pray:

- "Increase my love for You"
- "Remove what competes with You"
- "Teach me to desire You more than anything else"

But we do seek God to improve our circumstances, while leaving our devotion largely unchanged.

A prayer reset begins when we stop assuming we love God fully, and start praying intentionally for it. Until love for God becomes the focus of your prayers, it will not become the focus of your life.

Stop offering God partial devotion and start giving Him your whole heart without divided loyalties.

5. TRANSFORMATIONAL PRAYER

Father, You are worthy of all my love, yet I confess that my heart is often divided. I am drawn to my comfort and the concerns of daily life. I do not seek You as I should.

Teach me to love You with all my heart, soul, mind, and strength. Give me a desire for You that is greater than my desire for anything else. Help me to seek You first as the priority pursuit of my life.

Reveal anything to me that competes with You and give me the willingness to surrender it. Where my love is weak, strengthen it. Where my focus is scattered, bring it back to You.

Shape my heart so that I delight in Your presence, value Your Word, and choose obedience willingly. Let my life reflect a growing, wholehearted love for You, Almighty God.

6. SHORT ADDITIONAL PRAYERS

Teach Me to Seek You First
Lord, train my heart to come to You first in my thoughts, decisions, and daily life.

Remove Competing Loves
Father, give me courage to choose You above all else.

Help Me Delight in You
Lord, help me find real joy in Your presence and satisfaction in knowing You.

Strengthen My Obedience
Father, give me strength to obey You, even when it is difficult.

7. PERSONAL DIAGNOSTIC

1. What consistently occupies my thoughts more than God?
2. When I feel pressure, do I turn first to God, or something else?
3. Where do I consistently invest my time and attention?
4. What would be hardest to surrender if God asked?
5. What am I unwilling to give up, even if it competes with God?

What you see in these questions is already shaping your life. This is a matter of divided loyalty. What consistently holds first place will continue to direct your thinking and your responses, whether you acknowledge it or not.

The problem is not uncertainty. It is that what competes for your devotion has been allowed to remain in authority. What is not surrendered will continue to take priority, even when you intend otherwise.

This is where clarity must become action. Identify the one area where your devotion is not fully aligned and name it:

______________________________.

What is first in practice defines what is first in reality. Decide what will take first place tomorrow and act on it without delay.

My response:
I will bring my devotion back into alignment by

______________________________.

8. REAL-LIFE INTEGRATION

Loving God fully reshapes everyday life.

- It determines how you begin your day.
- It affects how you respond to difficulty.
- It guides your decisions.
- It shapes how you treat others.
- It influences what you pursue and what you let go.

When love for God grows trust becomes easier and priorities begin to shift. Love for God shows up in what you pursue, what you prioritize, and what you choose when there are competing interests. It is demonstrated by how your life is oriented during the day.

9. TAKE THIS STEP TODAY

Begin each day this week with a simple intentional prayer: "Lord, help me to love You more today than I did yesterday." Then act on it in one specific way:

- Give Him your first attention in the morning
- Turn to Him first in a moment of stress
- Choose obedience in one situation where it is difficult

Keep it simple, but consistent.

10. FINAL DECLARATION

I will give God my whole heart and remove every divided loyalty.

Chapter 2
KNOWING GOD DEEPLY

Prayers of Eternal Significance – Relationship and Awareness

1. REFRAME THE PRIORITY

Many people believe in God. Far fewer truly know Him. You may understand truths about God, attend church regularly, and maintain a consistent prayer habit, yet still lack a deep personal awareness of who He is. The ultimate gift of eternal life is not defined by activity or knowledge alone, but by knowing God in a real and growing relationship.

A prayer life of eternal significance must move beyond information about God to personal knowledge of God. Otherwise, prayer becomes routine and faith becomes distant.

2. WHAT THIS LOOKS LIKE

Knowing God deeply is relational and experiential. It means:

- Recognizing His character through experience.
- Listening as well as speaking in prayer.
- Responding to Him personally.
- Relating to Him as a present reality.

This kind of knowledge develops through consistent attention and intentional pursuit. You do not drift into knowing God, but rather you pursue Him intentionally.

3. EXPOSE THE GAP

Most believers say they know God, but they live with little awareness of Him. The real question is: How present is God in my daily awareness? Common patterns will reveal the gap:

- Prayer becomes a routine rather than a conversation
- Time with God is brief and inconsistent

- Awareness of God fades throughout the day
- Decisions are made without considering His input

You are not lacking knowledge. You are lacking awareness. A more serious problem is this: despite learning more about God you are becoming less aware of Him. Knowledge may be increasing, but intimacy is not.

We speak to God, but rarely slow down enough to engage Him. The problem is not rejection. The ultimate issue is the distance created by our inattention.

4. HOW TO PRAY DIFFERENTLY

When knowing God is not the goal, prayer becomes unfocused. We pray for guidance or provision because those are real and current issues in our life. But rarely do we pray:

- "Help me know You more intimately."
- "Make me aware of Your presence today."
- "Teach me to recognize Your work in my life."

Prayer has become functional instead of relational. We have not pursued knowing Him or sought a deeper relationship. A prayer reset shifts the focus from asking God to act to asking God to reveal Himself. This reorders and prioritizes them.

Knowing God does not occur automatically. It must be asked for, pursued, and practiced. You cannot know God deeply if you speak to Him only about your needs. If you do not seek to know God, you will continue to speak to Him without truly engaging Him.

Stop settling for surface-level knowledge of God and start pursuing a deep personal understanding of who He is.

5. TRANSFORMATIONAL PRAYER

Father, I acknowledge that I often know about You more than I truly know You. I move through prayer quickly and through my day with limited awareness of Your presence. I pray, but I do not always listen. I engage, but not very deeply.

Teach me to know You more fully. Help me to recognize You throughout my day and to respond to You personally. Slow me down so that I do not rush past opportunities to be with You.

Let my time with You become more than a daily habit or routine—make it real and meaningful. I surrender my tendency toward distraction and inattention. Draw me into a deeper relationship with You, where I not only believe in You, but walk with You.

6. SHORT ADDITIONAL PRAYERS

Make Me Aware of You
Lord, help me recognize Your presence throughout my day.

Teach Me to Listen
Father, quiet my thoughts so I hear and respond to You.

Deepen My Relationship with You
Lord, move me beyond routine and into a real and growing awareness of who You are.

Slow Me Down
Father, help me not to rush my time with You.

7. PERSONAL DIAGNOSTIC

1. Do I actually engage with God, or move quickly through time with Him?
2. How often am I aware of God throughout my day?
3. Do I pause to listen in prayer, or only speak?
4. What distractions prevent developing a deeper connection with God?
5. When was the last time I slowed down long enough that I recognized God's presence outside of my formal prayer time?

Your answers reveal if your relationship is really active. What you see here is shaping your life. This is not just a question of desire, but may illustrate busyness or apathy. What you give authority in your life will direct your thoughts, decisions, and the course of your life.

Identify one area where you are not totally engaged or where your devotion is not fully aligned and name it clearly. Do not generalize it or soften it. What is the real and underlying problem?

My response:
I will bring my devotion back into alignment by

______________________________.

8. REAL-LIFE INTEGRATION

Knowing God deeply affects how you live:

- It shapes how you make decisions.
- It influences how you respond to pressure.
- It affects how you view circumstances.
- It changes how you interact with others.

A person who knows God is more than informed—they are guided, aware, and responsive. Your daily awareness of God will determine how you live your day. What you practice in prayer will shape what you notice in life. If God is distant in prayer, He will likely feel distant in life.

9. TAKE THIS STEP TODAY

Pause for one minute at three different times during the day for the next week. In each pause:

- Acknowledge God's presence.
- Speak one sentence to Him.
- Remain silent briefly before moving on.

This practice builds awareness and attentiveness.

10. FINAL DECLARATION

I will pursue a deeper knowledge of God and not settle for surface understanding.

Chapter 3
SEEKING GOD FIRST

Prayers of Eternal Significance – Priority and Pursuit

1. REFRAME THE PRIORITY

Most people intend to seek God, but few actually make Him the central reality of their lives. God is included in your life, but not prioritized. He is not the beginning of it or the center of it. He might be consulted when difficulties arise, but He is not pursued regularly during the day.

A prayer life focused on prayers of eternal significance is created and shaped by priorities. What comes first shapes everything that follows. If God is not first and if He does not occupy the throne of your life, He will not be central in your family, work, or personal testimony.

2. WHAT THIS LOOKS LIKE

Seeking God first is a deliberate decision about priority, attention, and pursuit. It means:

- Desiring His direction more than your own plans.
- Pursuing Him consistently and continually.

Seeking God does not happen by accident. You must make a decision and follow through

3. EXPOSE THE GAP

Most believers say God should come first, but structure their lives otherwise. The real question is: Where does He actually fall in the order of your day? Common patterns reveal the gap:

- The day begins with tasks, not prayer.
- Time with God is delayed or shortened.
- Distractions are given immediate attention.
- Decisions are made quickly, with no godly reflection.

You are not openly rejecting God. You are postponing Him. A deeper issue exists: We say God is first, but we treat Him as unavailable. We intend to spend time with Him, but allow other priorities to take precedence. Over time, this becomes the normal pattern of life.

This is not a question of whether you value God. The issue is that you do not structure your life around that value. Passive neglect becomes your pattern.

4. HOW TO PRAY DIFFERENTLY

We pray after decisions are made, when problems arise, or when time allows. We rarely pray at the beginning: before decisions, before action, or before distraction. So prayer becomes secondary, and God becomes peripheral in practice.

A prayer reset changes the order. Instead of reacting in prayer, we begin with prayer. Instead of asking God to adjust our plans, we ask Him to shape them.

Seeking God first requires praying:

- "Order my day around You."
- "Help me come to You before anything else."
- "Train my mind to turn to You first."

Priority is not maintained simply by intentionality, but by practice reinforced through prayer. What you seek first will define what you become. If you do not begin with God, you will return to Him only when convenient.

Stop fitting God into your priorities and start building your life around Him as your foundation.

5. TRANSFORMATIONAL PRAYER

Father, I confess that I often intend to seek You, but allow other things to take Your place. I begin my day with tasks, distractions, and concerns. I come to You later, but only if time allows.

Teach me to reorder my priorities, and turn to You before anything else. Train my mind to seek You at the beginning of my day and before every decision.

Give me a desire for You that is stronger than my desire to move quickly to solutions. Help me slow down and acknowledge You.

I surrender my tendency to delay and my habit of distraction. Shape my daily rhythm so that You are at the center of my life. Let seeking You first become my pattern, not just my intention.

6. SHORT ADDITIONAL PRAYERS

Help Me Begin with You
Lord, train me to turn to You first at the start of my day.

Order My Priorities
Father, align my schedule and attention to Your priorities.

Redirect My Attention
Lord, when I am distracted, bring my focus back to You.

Shape My Decisions
Father, help me seek Your direction before I act.

7. PERSONAL DIAGNOSTIC

1. What gets my first attention each day? Is it God or something else?
2. What consistently takes priority over God?
3. In what areas am I assuming I will "get to God later" but rarely do?
4. What am I avoiding by staying busy instead of seeking God first?
5. Where have I decided something else is more urgent than God?"

Your answers identify what truly holds first place in your life, regardless of what you claim. Priority determines direction; what consistently comes first shapes every decision that you make. This exposes a habitual pattern where God is deferred rather than pursued, replaced by whatever feels urgent in the moment. What you put first is what you trust most. Choose one area where God is consistently second and change it now.

My response:

I will ______________________________.

8. REAL-LIFE INTEGRATION

Seeking God first is revealed in how you begin and how you respond. It is not measured by intention, but by order. It is revealed in:

- how it affects the start your day – what you do first.
- how it shapes how you approach decisions.
- how it influences how quickly you turn to Him under pressure.
- how you turn to God before other concerns.
- how you prioritize the decisions you bring to Him before you act.
- how you focus on Him when distractions arise.
- how you prioritize when time is limited.

When God is first, clarity increases. When He is not, life tends to be reactive. What you establish in prayer will determine what you prioritize in practice.

What you consistently choose first will shape the direction of your life.

9. TAKE THIS STEP TODAY

For the next seven days, begin your day with five uninterrupted minutes focused on God:

- Sit quietly.
- Acknowledge His presence.
- Speak one short prayer of surrender and direction.

Keep it simple, but consistent.

10. FINAL DECLARATION

I will make God my priority and order my life around Him.

Chapter 4
ABIDING IN CHRIST

Prayers of Eternal Significance – Daily Dependence

1. REFRAME THE PRIORITY

You may be trying to live *for* Christ without consistently living *with* Him. We focus on obedience and growth, yet overlook the one condition that makes all of those possible; remaining connected to Christ. Abiding is not an advanced concept for a few or the mature; it is the foundation for every disciple. Without it, effort increases while fruit decreases.

A prayer life built on eternal significance is not built on performance. It is formed by connection. What you remain connected to will determine what your life produces.

2. WHAT THIS LOOKS LIKE

Abiding in Christ is a continuous posture of dependence and awareness. It means:

- Relying on His strength rather than your own ability.
- Allowing His plans and teaching shape your thinking and responses.
- Being attentive to His presence.

Abiding is intentional. It is the repeated choice to remain connected and it must be maintained deliberately.

3. EXPOSE THE GAP

Most believers say abiding is important but do not practice it consistently. Common patterns reveal the gap:

- Time with God is limited to specific moments, not sustained awareness.

- Daily life is lived largely independent of conscious dependence on Christ.
- Prayer happens at set times, but connection fades between them.
- Effort replaces reliance when demands increase.

Effort is not the problem. You are lacking a relationship. The deeper issue is this: You try to produce spiritual results without maintaining the relationship. You attempt to be patient, wise, and faithful while functioning largely on our own strength. When pressure increases, you rely on effort instead of reconnecting. The problem is an intermittent relationship.

4. HOW TO PRAY DIFFERENTLY

If we do not abide, our prayer becomes compartmentalized. We pray at the beginning of the day, in moments of need, or at certain scheduled times. We rarely pray throughout the day. We don't say:

- "Keep me connected to You in this moment."
- "Help me return to You when I drift."
- "Remind me to depend on You, not myself."

Instead, we *believe* there is connection but *operate* independently. A prayer reset shifts from periodic prayer to and ongoing relationship expressed in prayer. Abiding requires intentional prayer such as:

- "Draw my attention back to You."
- "Teach me to return quickly when I drift."
- "Help me depend on You in this moment."

You remain connected by returning to Him continually in prayer. Depending on God is not weakness; it is the evidence of a relationship. If you return to God only at set times, you will continue to live most of your day independently.

Stop living independently of Christ and start remaining in constant dependence on Him throughout the day.

5. TRANSFORMATIONAL PRAYER

Father, I confess that I often try to live for You without staying closely connected. I begin with good intentions, but I drift into independence and rely on my own thinking and my own effort.

Teach me to remain in You. Help me to recognize when I am drifting. Remind me that I cannot produce lasting fruit apart from You.

In decisions, in pressure, and in ordinary moments, help me pause and reconnect. Strengthen my awareness of Your presence.

I surrender my tendency toward independence. I do not want to manage my life apart from You. Teach me to live in ongoing connection with You.

6. SHORT ADDITIONAL PRAYERS

Keep Me Connected
Lord, help me remain aware of You throughout my day.

Draw Me Back Quickly
Father, when I drift into independence or indifference, bring my attention back to You.

Teach Me Dependence
Lord, help me rely on You in each moment, not just in difficult times.

Guide My Thoughts and Actions
Father, direct my thinking as I stay connected to You.

7. PERSONAL DIAGNOSTIC

1. Do I rely on my own effort, or dependence on God?
2. How often do I return to Him during the day?

3. Where am I choosing self-reliance instead of staying connected to Christ?
4. Where am I choosing to trust myself over Christ?

Your answers show whether your day is lived in connection or in quiet separation. An abiding connection is not measured by moments of prayer but by how often and how seriously you return to Christ in the middle of ordinary decisions.

When attention drifts, reliance and self-direction begin to shape outcomes. This indicates a pattern of life where Christ is present in belief but absent in practice.

Address how you move through your day, not just how you begin it. What you do not return to, is not a priority. Decide when you will return to Christ during your day and follow through without exception.

My response:

I will ______________________________.

8. REAL-LIFE INTEGRATION

Abiding in Christ is revealed in ordinary moments. It is intentional. It is not about feelings or emotions, but rather the result of returning. You abide:

- In how you respond under pressure.
- In how you make decisions throughout the day.
- In how you handle interruptions and challenges.
- When you either pause or push forward on your own.
- By staying consciously connected to Christ.
- By responding to Him in real time.

You are abiding when you pause to acknowledge Him or bring decisions to Him. You are abiding when you direct your thoughts toward Him or depend on Him if problems arise.

But your connection will be tested in activity and busyness. If you feel connected to God only in quiet moments, your connection will be limited. If you practice seeking Him in active moments, your awareness will grow.

9. TAKE THIS STEP TODAY

For the next seven days, set a simple trigger to remind you to return to God throughout the day. Choose one recurring moment (for example: when you check your phone).

Each time the trigger occurs: pause briefly, acknowledge God's presence, and speak one short sentence to Him. Keep it simple, but consistent.

10. FINAL DECLARATION

I will remain in Christ daily and depend on Him for guidance.

Chapter 5
TRUSTING GOD COMPLETELY

Prayers of Eternal Significance – Confidence in His Ways

1. REFRAME THE PRIORITY

We say we trust God, but we still try to control the outcome. That becomes more difficult when outcomes are uncertain or not what we expected.

A prayer life focused on prayers of eternal significance must address this directly. Trust is not proven in what we say. It is revealed in how we respond. If trust is weak, prayer often becomes an attempt to manage life rather than surrender to His ways.

2. WHAT THIS LOOKS LIKE

Trusting God completely is a deliberate choice to rely on His provision. It means:

- Believing God is good when circumstances are not.
- Accepting His understanding is greater than yours.
- Releasing the need to control outcomes.
- Waiting without forcing a resolution.
- Obeying even when the result is uncertain.
- Choosing to rest in His care.

Trust is not passive, but rather it is active reliance. It shows up in what you do when you have doubts. It can be an issue in how you respond when plans change; in whether you trust Him or insist on control. The key to trusting Him is knowing you do not drift into trust, you choose it repeatedly.

3. EXPOSE THE GAP

Most believers trust God in principle but not in practice. For example:

- We pray for guidance but proceed with our own plans.
- We ask for help but continue to worry.
- We say we trust God but revisit concerns repeatedly.
- We look for reassurance rather than resting in His character.

You are not lacking belief; you are insisting on holding onto control. You trust God with your words, but not with outcomes. You want God's involvement, but still want your preferred result. So when things do not unfold as expected, your anxiety increases and you take control again.

You can pray sincerely and still live with persistent unease. The reason is because your trust has not been fully embedded in your relationship. You are choosing partial surrender.

4. HOW TO PRAY DIFFERENTLY

When trust is incomplete, our prayer reveals it. You pray:

- "Fix this situation."
- "Make this work out."
- "Give me the outcome I am hoping for."

These are natural—but they expose the problem. We are asking God to align with our plans rather than aligning ourselves with His. We rarely pray:

- "Help me trust You with the outcome."
- "Teach me to rest in Your character."
- "Give me peace even if the situation does not change."
- "Help me release control."

Our prayer becomes focused on securing results rather than strengthening trust. A prayer reset shifts from controlling through prayer to surrendering through prayer. Trust grows when prayer shifts from "change this" to "change how I respond" and "teach me to trust You in it." If your prayers are focused on outcomes, your trust will remain conditional.

Stop trusting your understanding of circumstances and start trusting God's character without reservation.

5. TRANSFORMATIONAL PRAYER

Father, I confess that I often say I trust You, but still try to control what happens. I hold onto outcomes, worry about what I cannot manage, and struggle when things do not go as I expect.

Teach me to trust You completely. Help me to rely on Your character, not on my understanding of the situation. When I feel uncertain, remind me that You know the plans You have for me.

Give me the strength to wait without forcing answers and to move forward in obedience even when the path is unclear.

I surrender my expectations and my desire for control. Teach me to rest in Your care and to trust You fully in every situation.

6. SHORT ADDITIONAL PRAYERS

Help Me Release Control

Lord, show me where I hold on too tightly and help me let go.

Strengthen My Confidence in You

Father, remind me of Your character when I feel uncertain.

Give Me Peace in Uncertainty
Lord, steady my thoughts when I cannot see the outcome.

Teach Me to Wait
Father, help me trust Your timing instead of forcing my own.

7. PERSONAL DIAGNOSTIC

1. What situation do I keep revisiting because I do not trust God with it?
2. Where am I expecting God's will to match what I already want?
3. Do my prayers reflect surrender or control?
4. When answers are delayed do I remain steady or become anxious?
5. What am I delaying because it requires obedience?
6. What am I unwilling to surrender if God asks?

Your responses reveal where trust breaks under pressure. What you revisit, control, or delay exposes where confidence in God has not been accepted. When trust is partial, anxiety begins to guide your responses.

This creates a cycle in which clarity is replaced by control. What is not trusted will be managed, and what is managed will not be surrendered. Identify one situation in which you are holding control and address it directly.

This will not resolve until trust replaces control. Decide where you will release control and act in alignment with that decision today.

My response:

I will ______________________________.

8. REAL-LIFE INTEGRATION

Trust is tested in uncertainty:

- When plans change unexpectedly.
- When outcomes are delayed.
- When decisions must be made without all the information.
- When circumstances do not improve as hoped.
- When you want to force a resolution.

Trust shows up in what you do in uncertainty. These are the moments in which trust becomes visible. What you practice in prayer will determine how you respond in these situations.

If you pray for trust, you will respond with steadiness. Trust is formed in repeated decisions to rely on God.

9. TAKE THIS STEP TODAY

Identify one current situation in which you feel uncertain or anxious. Each day this week:

- Name that situation specifically in prayer.
- Consciously release control of the outcome.
- Ask God for peace in that situation.

Return to the same situation each day and practice release.

10. FINAL DECLARATION

I will trust God's character even when I do not understand His ways.

Chapter 6
SURRENDERING TO GOD'S WILL

Prayers of Eternal Significance – Yielding Control

1. REFRAME THE PRIORITY

We ask God to guide our days then, hesitate when His plans challenge them. Surrender is assumed but rarely truly examined. It sounds simple in principle, yet it becomes difficult when God's direction conflicts with our personal preferences or expectations. Most believers want God's will but also want it to align with what they already desire.

Prayers of eternal significance require more than seeking direction. They require yielding to it. Our surrender is not proven when God agrees with us, but when He doesn't.

2. WHAT THIS LOOKS LIKE

Surrendering to God's will is the process and choice of yielding desires and plans to His authority. It means:

- Accepting that God's will is better than your own.
- Releasing your preferred outcomes when they conflict with His direction.
- Obeying even when the direction is uncertain.
- Trusting His timing instead of forcing your own.
- Letting His priorities reshape your ways.
- Being willing to adjust when He leads differently.

Surrender is active alignment. It shows up in decisions where your preferences are not followed. It might appear in situations where timing is delayed or in moments when obedience requires sacrifice. We choose to surrender repeatedly. It is not a one-time decision.

3. EXPOSE THE GAP

Most believers say they are willing to follow God's will – but attach conditions. These patterns reveal the gap:

- We seek God's direction but prefer a specific answer
- We delay obedience when His will is inconvenient
- We adjust His direction to fit our plans
- We move forward without clarity and call it faith

The problem is that you are not seeking God's will, you are negotiating with it. The issue is this: we want God's guidance without relinquishing control. We ask for His will but resist when it requires change. We are open in theory but selective in practice. Thus, you can pray sincerely and still resist.

4. HOW TO PRAY DIFFERENTLY

When surrender is incomplete, You pray:

- "Show me Your will."
- "Guide my decisions."
- "Help me know what to do."

These are good prayers but they stop short. You rarely pray:

- "Make me willing to accept Your will."
- "Help me release what I want if it is not Your plan."
- "Give me the strength to obey, even when it's costly."

Our prayers become focused on discovering God's will, rather than submitting to it. You must reset your prayer from seeking information to offering submission. Do not begin with "What do You want me to do?" Begin with "Prepare me to follow whatever You show me." Surrender is strengthened when prayer moves toward commitment. If you are not willing to follow, asking for direction changes nothing.

Stop asking God to oversee your plans and start yielding fully to His purposes.

5. TRANSFORMATIONAL PRAYER

Father, I confess that I often seek Your will while still holding onto my own. I want Your direction to align with what I have already decided.

Teach me to surrender fully to You. Help me to trust that Your will is better than mine. Give me the willingness to release my preferences and accept Your direction without resistance.

Prepare my heart to obey before I know what You will ask. Strengthen me to follow through and rest in Your authority.

I surrender my expectations, my timing, and my preferences. Shape my life according to Your will, not mine.

6. SHORT ADDITIONAL PRAYERS

Make Me Willing to Surrender
Lord, shape my heart so that I am ready to follow Your will.

Help Me Release My Plans
Father, give me the courage to let go of what I want when it conflicts with Your ways.

Strengthen My Obedience
Lord, help me act on what You put before me.

Align My Desires with Yours
Father, reshape what I want so that it reflects Your will.

7. PERSONAL DIAGNOSTIC

1. Where am I hoping God's will aligns with what I already want?

2. What have I delayed obeying because it is inconvenient or uncomfortable?
3. Do I ask for guidance knowing I will not follow through?
4. Where am I holding onto power instead of yielding it?
5. What am I avoiding because I suspect God may ask something different than what I want?

Delayed obedience is not a lack of understanding but a reluctance to yield when the cost is personal. When surrender is partial, obedience becomes selective. Your actions are shaped by preference rather than submission.

This pattern of holding on to control while asking for guidance keeps you from fully aligning with what God requires. Identify the one area where you are resisting surrender and name it directly.

Surrender is proven when control is released. What you do not yield will continue to govern you. Decide what you will yield now and act on it today.

My response:

I will ______________________________.

8. REAL-LIFE INTEGRATION

Surrender shows up in everyday decisions:

- When you choose obedience over convenience.
- When you accept timing you would not choose.
- When you follow through on what you know is right.
- When you release outcomes you cannot control.
- When you obey even when what is next is unknown.
- When you trust His timing instead of your own.

It shows up in decisions where your preferences are not followed. It might appear in situations when obedience requires sacrifice. These are the moments where surrender becomes visible.

What you pray for will shape how you respond. If you pray only for direction, you may hesitate. If you pray for surrender, you will move forward with increased confidence and commitment. Surrender is revealed in your actions.

9. TAKE THIS STEP TODAY

Identify one area where you sense resistance to God's direction. Each day this week:

- Name that area specifically in prayer.
- Acknowledge your resistance honestly.
- Ask God for willingness to surrender it.

Keep your focus on that one area until your response begins to change or feels aligned with His will.

10. FINAL DECLARATION

I will release control and submit fully to God's will.

Chapter 7
WORSHIPPING GOD REVERENTLY

Prayers of Eternal Significance – Honoring Who He is

1. REFRAME THE PRIORITY

We often come to God with our requests before acknowledging who He is. Prayer can begin quickly with needs and concerns while worship is brief or overlooked. Yet Scripture consistently presents worship, not requests, as the starting point. When honoring God is absent or shallow, everything that follows will be smaller and centered on self.

A prayer life focused on issues of eternal significance begins with a clear recognition of God's greatness. You will likely not pray rightly about your life until you see God as the Almighty Creator and Sustainer of all things.

2. WHAT THIS LOOKS LIKE

Worshipping God reverently is the act of honoring who He is: in His character, attributes, and works. It means:

- Reflecting on His attributes (e.g. holiness, power, wisdom, faithfulness)
- Recognizing His works in creation, history, or your life
- Letting your view of Him shape your perspective on everything else

Glorifying and uplifting God is what gives prayer its proper focus and foundation.

3. EXPOSE THE GAP

Most believers revere God, but it is often brief and shallow. Common patterns in personal worship reveal the gap:

- Reverence for God is reduced to familiar phrases.
- Prayer moves quickly from praise to requests.
- God is approached casually.
- Praise is very general.

You are not lacking reverence; you are just giving it too little attention. The deeper issue is we speak about God without truly considering His ways and desires. We use words of praise, but do not pause to reflect on their meaning. We say "You are great," but move on before that truth shapes our thinking. You may have a small view of God.

When our delight in God is shallow, problems feel larger, anxiety increases, and prayer becomes centered on self. The issue is the lack of a true understanding of His greatness.

4. HOW TO PRAY DIFFERENTLY

When your delight in God is minimal, your prayer becomes unbalanced. You pray for help, provision, and solutions, but give little attention to The Provider. You spend little time reflecting on God's character or acknowledging His greatness. You rarely pray:

- "Help me see You more clearly."
- "Remind me of who You are before I ask for anything."
- "Expand my understanding of Your greatness."

A prayer reset changes where you begin. Instead of beginning with requests we should begin with focusing on God. We must allow our reverence for God to shape everything that follows. Recognizing the power and love of God should reorder how you perceive your needs. Worship that costs nothing changes nothing. If you do not begin with a focus on God, your prayers will remain centered on yourself.

Stop approaching God casually and start honoring Him for who He truly is.

5. TRANSFORMATIONAL PRAYER

Father, I acknowledge that I come to You quickly with my needs. I speak words of praise but do not always reflect on their meaning. My view of You is too small and my focus too narrow.

Help me to see You more clearly. Teach me to recognize Your greatness, holiness, and power. Remind me of Your faithfulness so that my understanding of You grows deeper.

Give me a greater awareness of who You are before I focus on what I need. I surrender my tendency toward shallow attention. Expand my view of You so that my prayer, my perspective, and my life are shaped by who You truly are.

6. SHORT ADDITIONAL PRAYERS

Help Me See You Clearly
Lord, expand my understanding of Your greatness.

Remind Me of Your Works
Father, bring to mind what You have done so I do not overlook Your attributes.

Slow Me Down in Worship
Lord, keep me from rushing past Your faithfulness.

Deepen My Reverence
Father, teach me to approach You with honor and humility.

7. PERSONAL DIAGNOSTIC

1. What does my worship reveal about how I see God?
2. Are my expressions of worship specific or repetitive?
3. Do I pause long enough to consider who God is?
4. Is my view of God large or limited?
5. What am I avoiding by keeping worship brief and moving quickly to my concerns?

Your answers reveal how you actually approach God. When worship is secondary, your view of God is reduced. Your prayers shift toward your needs rather than His worth. This exposes a pattern of approaching God with familiarity and not reverence.

A lower view of God leads to diminished worship, which shapes every other part of your prayer life. Identify where you avoid honoring Him and address that pattern directly.

How you worship reveals how you see God. Decide where you will intentionally slow down and honor God for who He is before asking anything.

My response:

I will ____________________________.

8. REAL-LIFE INTEGRATION

Honoring God shapes how you see everything:

- It affects how you respond to problems.
- It influences your level of anxiety or peace.
- It shapes your confidence in uncertainty.
- It determines whether your focus is on God or on circumstances.
- It indicates your level of respect and reverence.

Reverent worship is not about emotional intensity. It is the clear recognition of the holy sovereign God who created all things. It is expressed through what you say about God and how you approach Him.

When your view of God is clear, problems become smaller in comparison. When you have a limited view of God, your problems feel overwhelming.

What you consistently acknowledge in prayer will shape what you focus on in life. If you practice worship with humility, you will carry that perspective into daily decisions and actions.

9. TAKE THIS STEP TODAY

For the next seven days begin each prayer time by focusing on one specific attribute or work of God. Before making any requests, name it clearly (for example: His faithfulness), speak 2–3 sentences about it, and reflect briefly on what it means to you. Be specific and intentional.

10. FINAL DECLARATION

I will honor God with reverence and heartfelt worship.

Chapter 8
THANKING GOD IN ALL THINGS

Prayers of Eternal Significance – Practicing Gratitude

1. REFRAME THE PRIORITY

We are quick to ask God for what we lack but slow to thank Him for what He has given. Gratitude should be a major part of prayer. Scripture repeatedly calls us to give thanks. Thanksgiving should occur consistently in our daily life, not just in favorable circumstances.

This is not natural to most people. It requires a shift in how we see our lives and how we see God. Our prayer and quiet time must begin by recognizing what God has done in all parts of our life.

2. WHAT THIS LOOKS LIKE

Thanking God in all things goes beyond a polite prayer of acknowledgment. It becomes a disciplined posture of the heart. It means:

- Recognizing God as the source of all good.
- Remembering what He has already done.
- Acknowledging His presence in both the good times and bad.
- Valuing what is eternal over what will not last.

This does not mean we pretend everything is good. It means we trust that God is good in the times that are challenging, even in the times when life seems to be at its lowest. Why is that? How can that be? Because our gratitude is not based on our circumstances, it is rooted in God's character and works.

3. EXPOSE THE GAP

Most believers give thanks, but only selectively and briefly. We are usually most grateful:

- When something goes well.
- When a prayer is answered as expected.
- When life feels stable.

In difficulty our gratitude fades or disappears. Complaints increase when the focus shifts to what is missing. We rarely stop to recognize how consistently God is providing, sustaining, and working in ways we overlook or cannot see.

We receive from God constantly, yet remain unaware of it. When gratitude is absent, our perspective narrows. We begin to see life primarily through problems rather than through God's provision.

4. HOW TO PRAY DIFFERENTLY

When gratitude is not present, your prayers become request-driven. You pray: "Help me..." or "Fix this..." These are not wrong, but they are just not on target. You rarely pray:

- "Thank You for what You have already done."
- "Thank You for what I do not yet understand."
- "Thank You for Your presence in this situation."

Without gratitude, prayer becomes centered on what is missing rather than what has already been given. A prayer reset means intentionally shifting from request-driven prayer to recognition-based prayer. Gratitude reorders our focus.

It is not a response to circumstances, it corrects our perspective. If we thank God only when circumstances change, our gratitude will remain shallow.

Stop thanking God only when life goes well and start giving thanks in every circumstance.

5. TRANSFORMATIONAL PRAYER

Father, You have given me far more than I recognize. I confess that I focus on what I lack rather than what You have provided. I move slowly to gratitude.

Teach me to see Your hand in my life more clearly. Help me to remember Your faithfulness and provision in every season. When circumstances are difficult, remind me that You are still in charge and at work.

Give me a heart that thanks You for all things. Let gratitude shape my perspective, my words, and my prayers. Help me to live with a constant awareness of all that You have done and are doing in my life.

6. SHORT ADDITIONAL PRAYERS

Thank You for What I Overlook
Lord, open my eyes to the blessings I take for granted.

Thank You in Difficulty
Father, even in this situation, I thank You.

Thank You for Who You Are
God, I thank You for being faithful, good, and unchanging.

Thank You Before the Outcome
Lord, I thank You in advance, trusting that You are working even when I cannot see it.

7. PERSONAL DIAGNOSTIC

1. Do I thank God as often as I ask Him for help?
2. Do I thank God in difficulty or only when life is good?
3. What have I received that I have not acknowledged?

4. Do my prayers reflect awareness of His past faithfulness?
5. What does my prayer life reveal about what I value most?

Your answers show what you notice and what you overlook. Gratitude reflects awareness. If it is absent, your focus narrows to what is lacking rather than what has been given.

When gratitude is conditional, your perspective will be unstable and easily shaped by changing outcomes. What you fail to acknowledge will eventually be forgotten, even if it was once clear. Identify where gratitude is missing and bring it into focus intentionally.

What you consistently acknowledge will shape what you see. Decide what you will begin acknowledging daily.

My response:

I will ______________________________.

8. REAL-LIFE INTEGRATION

Gratitude changes how you live, not just how you pray:

- It affects how you respond to inconvenience and stress.
- It shapes your attitude toward people and circumstances.
- It influences your contentment and peace.
- It steadies you in uncertainty.

What you consistently notice in life will shape what you consistently say in prayer. A grateful person sees life differently because God is more visible. When gratitude grows, complaint diminishes, and trust becomes much easier.

9. TAKE THIS STEP TODAY

For the next seven days, begin each prayer time with this discipline: Before making any requests, list three specific things you thank God for.

Keep them specific, not general. Repeat this daily. It will begin to retrain your focus.

10. FINAL DECLARATION

I will give thanks to God in every circumstance.

Chapter 9
LIVING FOR GOD'S GLORY

Prayers of Eternal Significance – God-Centered Purpose

1. REFRAME THE PRIORITY

Most people want a meaningful life, but few define it in terms of God's glory. In our faith life we focus on personal spiritual growth and God's blessing. Yet Scripture consistently points beyond self to a greater purpose. Our mission is to live in a way that reflects and honors God.

Prayers of eternal significance address this shift. If the goal remains centered on self, even spiritual activity can become limited. When the goal becomes God's glory, everything will begin to align.

2. WHAT THIS LOOKS LIKE

Living for God's glory means you orient your life around honoring Him. It means:

- Viewing success in terms of faithfulness to Him, not recognition by others.
- Letting God's reputation matter more than your own.

You do not live for God's glory by accident. You must choose it deliberately.

3. EXPOSE THE GAP

Most believers say life should honor God, but their decisions reflect something else. Common patterns reveal that gap:

- Decisions are based primarily on convenience or personal preference.
- Success is measured by personal advancement rather than spiritual faithfulness.
- Attention is drawn toward self rather than God.

We are not necessarily ignoring God, but rather we are centering on ourselves. The deeper issue is that we want God to be involved in our lives, but not central to our purpose. We ask for His help or guidance but still evaluate life based on our own needs and wants.

You can live a disciplined active life and still be driven by personal goals. The question is focus and priority. The issue is what your life is oriented around.

4. HOW TO PRAY DIFFERENTLY

When your attention is on yourself, your prayers reflect it because you will pray:

- "Help me succeed."
- "Bless what I am doing."
- "Give me the outcome I want."

These are inadequate because you rarely pray:

- "Be honored in what I do."
- "Use this situation for Your plans, not just mine."
- "Help me pursue what matters most to You."

A prayer reset shifts from self-centered requests to God-centered alignment. Stop asking God to support your plans, and ask Him to reshape your purpose. Living for God's glory requires prayer that asks "How does this reflect God?" Your object must be to honor Him in what you do. If God's glory is not your aim in prayer, it will not be your aim in life.

Stop living for your own outcomes and start living for what brings God the greatest glory.

5. TRANSFORMATIONAL PRAYER

Father, I confess that I focus on my own goals and desires more than on Your glory. I do not always consider whether my life is truly reflecting You.

Redirect my thinking so that I evaluate decisions based on what reflects You and not just what benefits me.

Give me the clarity to recognize when my focus has shifted back to myself. Help me choose faithfulness over recognition and obedience over convenience. I surrender my desire for control and approval. Align my life with Your plans.

6. SHORT ADDITIONAL PRAYERS

Align My Purpose with Yours
Lord, help me pursue what matters to You, not me.

Be Honored in My Decisions
Father, guide my choices so they reflect Your priorities.

Shift My Focus from Self to You
Lord, redirect my thinking when I become centered on my own outcomes.

Strengthen My Faithfulness
Father, help me choose obedience.

7. PERSONAL DIAGNOSTIC

1. What actually drives my decisions? Is it God's glory or personal benefit?
2. Do I define success by results or by faithfulness to God's precepts?
3. Where am I seeking recognition instead of reflecting His character?

4. What decision am I making that is centered on me instead of Him?

Your answers reveal what ultimately drives your decisions. If your personal benefit takes priority, your direction shifts toward yourself, even if your intention is otherwise. This creates a pattern in which the purpose becomes self-centered rather than God-centered.

What you aim for determines how you act, and over time, that direction becomes fixed. What you pursue determines what your life produces. If this does not change, your direction will remain centered on yourself.

Identify the decision where your focus is misaligned and address it directly. Decide what you will pursue for God's glory and act on that decision now.

My response:

I will ______________________________.

8. REAL-LIFE INTEGRATION

Living for God's glory is revealed in everyday choices:

- In how you handle success and failure.
- In how you respond when you are overlooked.
- In how you carry out responsibilities.
- In whether your actions point to God or to yourself.
- In whether your decisions reflect His character and priorities.
- In whether you seek outcomes that point to Him or yourself.
- In whether you represent Him faithfully in your relationships and responsibilities.
- In whether you choose obedience even when it goes unnoticed.

This can be very practical because it appears in how you respond when no one is watching. It is seen in what happens when you are under stress, or what you prioritize when alternative options compete.

This is not limited to major decisions, but rather it includes ordinary moments as well. What you consistently pray for will influence how you live. If your prayers center on God's glory, your decisions will begin to align with that purpose.

9. TAKE THIS STEP TODAY

Choose one area of your life where decisions are frequent (relationships, for example). Each day this week, before making a decision in that area: pause briefly, ask: "What would honor God most here?" and let that question shape your response. Keep the focus consistent and intentional.

10. FINAL DECLARATION

I will live for God's glory instead of my own outcomes.

PART 2 – PRAYERS FOR OTHERS

Strengthening the Body of Christ

This section has one purpose: to move your focus from yourself to others and identify your responsibility toward what the Bible describes as "one another."

Prayer can easily turn inward. You naturally bring your personal needs, concerns, and situations to Him. But left there, prayer becomes limited. You may care about others in thought, but not in action.

The life of a believer is not lived in isolation. It is revealed in relationships: in how you love, engage, and take responsibility for others. If you are not praying for others, you will not stay engaged with them. When you disengage, relationships weaken.

Prayer is where concern becomes intentional and where awareness becomes action.

If you do not pray for others, you will not invest in them. And what you do not invest in will not grow.

Begin and engage here!

Chapter 10
LOVING ONE ANOTHER

Prayers of Eternal Significance – Sacrificial Care

1. REFRAME THE PRIORITY

You can say you love God while you consistently struggle to love others. Love for others is not secondary in the Christian life, because it is one of the clearest evidences of true discipleship. Yet, it is treated as an ideal rather than a daily commitment. We value relationships but still respond with impatience or indifference when it matters most.

A prayer life using prayers of eternal significance must address this directly. You cannot pursue a God-centered life while neglecting the people God has placed around you. How you treat others is not separate from your spiritual life. It is a reflection of it!

2. WHAT THIS LOOKS LIKE

Loving one another is the choice to act with patience, humility, and affection. It is:

- an internal choice to love regardless of feeling
- an intentional posture
- an definition of sacrificial love

This is not emotional or romantic devotion. It is expressed through intentionality and action. You may say you love others, but you must practice it consistently.

3. EXPOSE THE GAP

Most believers say love matters, but do not apply it consistently. Common patterns expose this gap:

- We are impatient with some people.

- We withdraw when relationships become difficult.
- We react too quickly when offended.
- We prioritize our own time, comfort, and preferences.

You are not unwilling to love, but you are selective in who you adore. The deeper issue is this: you expect grace from others in your weakness, but withdraw that grace when they fail you. You justify your responses based on how others act. You wait for them to change before you adjust your behavior. Relationship becomes conditional, shaped by the actions of others rather than by a commitment to love unconditionally.

You may speak about affection and still live in ways that are guarded, reactive, and self-protective. The issue is how you apply that love.

4. HOW TO PRAY DIFFERENTLY

When love is inconsistent, your prayers reveal it. You pray:

- "Change them."
- "Fix this relationship."
- "Help them understand."

These prayers focus on others, but avoid responsibility. You rarely pray:

- "Change how I respond to them."
- "Help me act with patience and humility."
- "Show me where I am contributing to the problem."
- "Give me the willingness to love even if it is not returned."

Our prayer becomes a way to manage others rather than transform ourselves. A prayer reset shifts the focus from asking God to adjust others to asking God to shape our response. Instead of praying "make this easier," pray "make me faithful in how I love." If your prayers are focused on changing others, your love will remain conditional.

Stop loving others conditionally
and start loving them sacrificially
as Christ has loved you.

5. TRANSFORMATIONAL PRAYER

Father, I confess that I do not always care about others as I should. I am patient when it is easy, but I become frustrated or self-focused when relationships are difficult.

I expect others to change, while overlooking my own responses. Teach me to love consistently. Help me to act with humility and kindness.

Shape my words so they build up rather than tear down. Help me forgive quickly and remain engaged rather than withdraw. I surrender my desire to be right, to be comfortable, and to be affirmed. Teach me to love others in a way that reflects You.

6. SHORT ADDITIONAL PRAYERS

Help Me Respond with Patience
Lord, give me control over my reactions.

Teach Me to Forgive
Father, help me release offenses instead of holding onto them.

Strengthen My Commitment to Love
Lord, help me act well and with consistency.

Guard My Words
Father, guide what I say so that it encourages others.

7. PERSONAL DIAGNOSTIC

1. Who am I choosing not to love because it costs me?
2. How do I respond when I feel wronged?
3. Do I expect others to change more than I expect myself to change?
4. Where have I withdrawn instead of engaging?
5. What am I avoiding because loving this person would require effort or humility?

Your responses reveal where your love is limited by certain conditions or responses. If love is withheld or dependent on others, relationships become shaped by self-protection rather than love. This exposes a pattern of expecting change from others, but resisting it yourself.

Love that is measured or controlled will not reflect Christ and will not produce lasting change. What you withhold will define the relationship more than what you give. Identify any person or situation where love is being restricted and address it directly. Decide how you will act toward this person and follow through without delay.

My response:

I will ______________________________.

8. REAL-LIFE INTEGRATION

Loving one another means:

- Choosing to act with kindness, even if it is not returned.
- Being patient when others are slow to change.
- Putting the needs of others ahead of my convenience.
- Speaking in ways that build up rather than tear down.
- Forgiving when you have been wronged.
- Remaining engaged rather than withdrawing.

Loving one another is lived out in ordinary everyday moments. It reveals itself in how you respond during disagreements and treat people who inconvenience you. It can be seen in whether you listen or react.

Love shows up in daily interactions, small decisions, and repeated acts. It is not really tested in ideal conditions. Love is revealed in difficult times when it would be easy to focus on yourself. What you pray about relationships will shape how you act within those connections.

If your prayers focus on changing others, you will remain reactive. If your prayers focus on your own faithfulness, your actions will become more effective. Love will become visible in repeated everyday choices.

9. TAKE THIS STEP TODAY

Identify one relationship where your love has been inconsistent. Each day this week (1) pray specifically for your own actions in that relationship, and (2) choose one deliberate act of patience, kindness, or engagement.

Keep your focus on your actions, not theirs.

10. FINAL DECLARATION

I will love others sacrificially as Christ has loved me.

Chapter 11
LIVING IN UNITY

Prayers of Eternal Significance – Harmony and Oneness

1. REFRAME THE PRIORITY

You assume unity exists but rarely work to preserve it. Relationships within the body of Christ are meant to reflect something greater than agreement or compatibility. Unity is not the absence of differences; it is the presence of a shared commitment to Christ that overrides them.

A prayer life built on a foundation of eternity must recognize that harmony and agreement in the church is not automatic. Unity is intentional and when it is neglected, division results.

2. WHAT THIS LOOKS LIKE

Living in unity is the choice to pursue harmony and a shared purpose. Differences may exist but they are set aside for the common good. It means:

- shared commitment.
- agreement over difference.
- internal decision to prioritize relationship.

You refuse to turn minor issues into major division.

3. EXPOSE THE GAP

Most believers say they value unity but their responses create division. Common situations reveal the gap:

- We withdraw when relationships become difficult.
- We defend our position rather than seek compromise or understanding.
- We allow small offenses rather than pursue resolution.

- We avoid conversations that could lead to resolution.
- We take a stand on an insignificant issue way beyond its importance.

You are not protecting truth; you are protecting your position. The deeper issue is that you protect your position, even when it breaks the connection in the relationship. You justify your perspective and protect your position by calling it "standing firm." But it comes at the cost of unity.

4. HOW TO PRAY DIFFERENTLY

When unity is strained, your prayers will reveal your position. We pray "change them" or "help them see my point" or "fix this situation." These prayers focus on resolution, but avoid responsibility.

You rarely pray:

- "Show me where I need to change."
- "Help me pursue unity even when it is difficult."
- "Give me humility in this situation."
- "Help me take the first step toward reconciliation."

Prayer can become focused on correcting others instead of aligning yourself. A prayer reset shifts from defending a position to pursuing harmony. Instead of asking God to resolve the conflict externally, you begin asking Him to shape our response internally.

Unity is strengthened when prayer shifts from expectation to responsibility. Harmony is not maintained by agreement, but by alignment. If you are not willing to take responsibility, unity will not be restored.

Stop allowing division to take root and start actively pursuing unity in Christ.

5. TRANSFORMATIONAL PRAYER

Father, I confess that I do not always pursue unity as I should. I hold onto my perspective and avoid the effort required to maintain connection. I want resolution without taking responsibility.

Teach me to value harmony more deeply. Help me choose humility over being right, and connection over convenience.

Give me the courage to take the first step when needed. Help me to listen, to understand, and to respond with patience.

I surrender my need to be justified and my reluctance to engage. Shape my actions so that I pursue unity actively.

6. SHORT ADDITIONAL PRAYERS

Give Me Humility
Lord, help me release the need to be right.

Help Me Pursue Peace
Father, give me the courage to move toward resolution.

Guard My Words
Lord, guide my words so I promote unity not foster division.

Strengthen My Commitment to Unity
Father, help me remain engaged even when it is difficult.

7. PERSONAL DIAGNOSTIC

1. Where am I choosing distance instead of engagement in the work of unity?
2. Do I prioritize being understood more than understanding others?

3. What relationship am I avoiding because harmony would require effort?
4. What am I justifying that is contributing to division?
5. Where am I justifying behavior that creates division?

Your responses reveal if you are not engaged in pursuing unity. When you require being understood, division is easily sustained. Are you protecting your position rather than doing the work required for harmony?

Division does not remain isolated; it shapes how you relate to others and how you respond when conflict arises. Unity requires intentional effort from you. If you do not pursue it, division will continue to define the relationship.

Decide where you will take the first step toward unity and act on it without delay. Identify the relationship where you are allowing distance to remain and address it directly.

My response:

I will ______________________________.

8. REAL-LIFE INTEGRATION

Unity means:

- Valuing relationship over personal preference.
- Choosing humility instead of insisting on being right.
- Seeking understanding before reacting.
- Maintaining peace rather than escalating conflict.
- Working toward resolution rather than withdrawing.
- Prioritizing what unites over what divides.

It does not mean avoiding disagreement or suppressing truth. It means handling differences in a way that preserves relationships and reflects Christ. Unity is visible in how you respond when tension arises.

What you pray about relationships will shape how you act within them. If your prayers focus on others changing, your responses will be guarded. If your prayers focus on your responsibility, your actions will become more intentional.

Unity is maintained by intention and sustained through consistent action.

9. TAKE THIS STEP TODAY

Identify one relationship where there is tension, distance, or unresolved conflict. This week:

- Pray specifically for your role in that situation.
- Take one intentional step toward connection, a conversation, a message, or an act of engagement.

Focus on your action, not the outcome.

10. FINAL DECLARATION

I will pursue unity and refuse to contribute to division.

Chapter 12
ENCOURAGING OTHERS

Prayers of Eternal Significance – Strengthening Faith

1. REFRAME THE PRIORITY

We tend to assume encouragement will happen natural. It rarely does. Most people are aware of the need to support others, yet daily life moves quickly and opportunities pass without any action. Encouragement becomes occasional rather than intentional. Silence replaces anything being done.

Prayers of eternal significance must address words and actions that build others up. Words and actions shape faith and affect endurance. What you choose to say or not say has more impact than you may realize.

2. WHAT THIS LOOKS LIKE

Encouraging others is the act of strengthening someone's faith and perspective. That can include:

- specific encouragement or providing clarity.
- an internal posture of attentiveness.
- building others up deliberately.

3. EXPOSE THE GAP

Most believers value encouragement, but practice it inconsistently. Common patterns reveal the gap:

- We think positive things about others but do not express them.
- We believe people know what we appreciate.

- We hesitate to speak because it feels unnecessary or awkward.
- We focus on worldly problems rather than faith.

You are not unaware, you are inactive. The deeper issue is that you see what could strengthen others but leave it unsaid. You delay or minimize the moment. What could have strengthened someone is left unspoken. Over time, this becomes a pattern of passive neglect.

It is possible to care about people and still leave them unsupported. The problem is the absence of deliberate action.

4. HOW TO PRAY DIFFERENTLY

When encouragement is not intentional, your prayers reflect it. You pray "help them" or "strengthen them" or "be with them." These prayers are good but incomplete.
You rarely pray:

- "Use me to strengthen them today."
- "Show me what they need to hear."
- "Give me the courage to speak up if I hesitate."
- "Make me attentive to opportunities to help others."

When encouragement remains general instead of personal, we need to shift from asking God to act to have Him work through you. Instead of praying "take care of them" pray "position me to strengthen them."

Encouragement increases when prayer moves from observation to participation. Words shape faith more than we realize. If you are not willing to act, your encouragement will remain unspoken.

Stop withholding encouragement and start strengthening others with words and actions.

5. TRANSFORMATIONAL PRAYER

Father, I confess that I see opportunities to encourage others but do not act on them. I think positive things, but often remain silent. Help me to act when I see the need, not after it is too late. Shape my speech so that it consistently builds up.

Teach me to be purposeful in building others up. Help me to notice what others need and to respond with clarity and courage. Give me the words that strengthen the faith of others and the awareness to recognize the right moments to speak.

I surrender my passivity and distraction. Use me to strengthen others in ways that are timely and meaningful.

6. SHORT ADDITIONAL PRAYERS

Make Me Attentive
Lord, help me notice and act on the needs of others.

Give Me the Right Words
Father, guide what I say so that it strengthens and encourages.

Remove My Hesitation
Lord, help me act when I see the opportunity.

Use Me to Build Others Up
Father, position me to strengthen the faith of others.

7. PERSONAL DIAGNOSTIC

1. How often do I stay silent when I should speak?
2. What keeps me from speaking when I know I should?
3. Where have I noticed a need but failed to respond?
4. What am I avoiding by remaining silent when encouragement is needed?

5. In what situations am I choosing silence instead of strengthening someone?

Your replies show where you recognize the need but fail to act. When encouragement is withheld, opportunities to strengthen others are lost, and silence becomes a pattern. What is left unsaid cannot build up anyone, and over time, that absence weakens those around you.

What you do not say cannot strengthen anyone. If you remain silent, the opportunity is lost. Identify the moment where you choose silence and address it directly. Decide when you will speak and follow through without hesitation.

My response:

I will ____________________________.

8. REAL-LIFE INTEGRATION

Effective encouragement means:

- Speaking in ways that give clarity and hope.
- Recognizing and affirming what is good and faithful.
- Reminding others of truth when they are discouraged.
- Offering support rather than remaining silent.
- Choosing words that strengthen rather than weaken.
- Being attentive to what others actually need.

Encouragement should not be vague. It should be specific and purposeful. It is seen in what you choose to say and whether you act when the opportunity is present.

These are not rare opportunities, but rather they are frequent and often missed. What you pray about will shape what you do. If you pray generally, you will respond generally. If you pray for specific awareness and responses, you will begin to engage more intentionally.

9. TAKE THIS STEP TODAY

Each day this week encourage one specific person.

- Identify the person ahead of time.
- Speak to them or write a personal note that builds them up.
- Do not delay; act when the opportunity arises.

Keep it simple and consistent.

10. FINAL DECLARATION

I will intentionally encourage others in order to strengthen their faith.

Chapter 13
BEARING OTHER'S BURDENS

Prayers of Eternal Significance – Shared Struggle

1. REFRAME THE PRIORITY

We care about people's struggles but keep a comfortable distance from becoming involved in them. It is appropriate to express concern, offer quick support, or say we will pray. But bearing someone's burden requires more than awareness.

Prayers focused on eternal significance must address this difference. Compassion that does not act is incomplete. If we are unwilling to enter into the struggles of others, we reduce Christ-likeness to observation rather than participation.

2. WHAT THIS LOOKS LIKE

Bearing one another's burdens is the choice to step into another's struggle and help carry it. It is reflected in:

- becoming actively involved.
- real commitment vs casual concern.
- an internal willingness to engage.

You bear burdens by entering into them deliberately.

3. EXPOSE THE GAP

Most believers express compassion, but stop short of doing something. Certain patterns reveal the gap:

- We say "I'll pray for you," but do not follow through.
- We listen briefly but move on quickly.

- We offer encouragement without understanding the depth of the situation.
- We avoid ongoing involvement because it requires time and energy.

You are not lacking compassion; you are avoiding being involved. You fear the inconvenience or the uncertainty of how to help. You keep your distance while maintaining a sense of care.

You can be aware of a struggle and still leave someone to carry it alone. You may have genuine concern or compassion but are unwilling to engage.

4. HOW TO PRAY DIFFERENTLY

When your involvement is limited, your prayers reflect it. You pray "help them" or "be with them." These prayers are nice but they remain distant. You rarely pray:

- "Show me how to help carry this burden."
- "Give me the willingness to stay engaged."
- "Help me be consistent in supporting them."
- "Use me in a meaningful way in their situation."

Prayer can become a substitute for involvement rather than of preparation for it. A prayer reset shifts from observation to engagement. Instead of praying "take care of them," pray "position me to walk with them."

Burden-bearing increases when prayer moves from general concern to personal responsibility. Burdens shared in prayer are no longer carried alone. If you are not willing to engage, your prayers will remain relatively distant.

Stop remaining distant from others' struggles and start entering into them with compassion.

5. TRANSFORMATIONAL PRAYER

Father, I confess that I often see the struggles of others but do not fully step into them. I feel concern, but I hesitate to become involved.

Teach me to bear the burdens of others faithfully. Give me the willingness to stay engaged, even when it is difficult or costly.

Show me how to help in ways that are meaningful and consistent. Remove my tendency to keep a distance and replace it with involved compassion.

I surrender my desire for comfort and convenience. Use me to support others. Let my actions reflect genuine care, not just momentary concern.

6. SHORT ADDITIONAL PRAYERS

Make Me Willing to Engage
Lord, help me step into the needs of others.

Show Me How to Help
Father, give me clarity in how I can provide real help.

Strengthen My Consistency
Lord, help me remain involved.

Give Me Compassion That Acts
Father, move me from concern to meaningful action.

7. PERSONAL DIAGNOSTIC

1. When someone shares a burden, do I engage or step away?
2. Do I follow through after I say I will help?
3. Where do I remove myself because involvement is costly?

4. What holds me back from staying engaged?
5. What am I avoiding by offering words instead of practical support?

Your answers indicate how you respond when involvement is challenging. When you step back or fail to follow through, others carry their struggles alone. This produces an ongoing sequence in which support is offered in words but not sustained in action. What you avoid becomes distance, and that distance limits the depth of your relationships.

Consistent engagement is what carries burdens, not occasional involvement. Identify situations where you withdraw when it becomes difficult and address that pattern directly. What you do not carry with others, they carry alone. Decide where you will remain engaged and follow through consistently.

My response:

I will ______________________________.

8. REAL-LIFE INTEGRATION

Burden-bearing is practiced in ongoing situations such as.

- Taking time to understand what someone is facing.
- Remaining engaged when situations are difficult.
- Offering practical help, even if inconvenient.
- Sharing the emotional weight by listening and support.
- Praying consistently and specifically for their need.
- Continuing support over time, not just in the moment.
- Following through after the initial conversation.

These are the moments that define real commitment. What you pray about others' struggles will shape how you respond. If your prayers remain general, your involvement will remain limited. If your prayers include engagement, your actions will become more consistent.

9. TAKE THIS STEP TODAY

Identify one person who is currently carrying a significant burden. This week:

- Reach out intentionally (call, message, or meet).
- Ask one thoughtful question and listen carefully.
- Follow up at least once after the initial conversation.

Focus on consistency, not complexity.

10. FINAL DECLARATION

I will enter into the struggles of others and walk with them.

Chapter 14
FORGIVING AND RECONCILING

Prayers of Eternal Significance – Restored Relationships

1. REFRAME THE PRIORITY

We want peace in relationships but we resist the cost required to restore them when necessary. Forgiveness and reconciliation are central to the Christian life, yet they are often delayed or avoided. Offense can feel justified and creating distance seems safer. But, unresolved conflict does not remain neutral, because it shapes attitudes, hardens responses, and limits spiritual growth.

A prayer life focused on eternal significance will address this directly. You cannot pursue a restored relationship with God while consistently avoiding restored relationships with others. Loving others should always be a priority.

2. WHAT THIS LOOKS LIKE

Forgiving and reconciling is the choice to release offense and pursue restoration. It includes a distinction between forgiveness (internal) and reconciliation (relational).

Forgiveness is the practice of internally releasing an offense. Forgiveness is not based on feelings; it is chosen deliberately. This is personal and has relatively little to do with the other party involved.

Reconciliation, on the other hand, is relational. It is the process of restoring the connection. Both require humility, willingness, and intentional action.

3. EXPOSE THE GAP

Most believers acknowledge forgiveness but hesitate to practice it. Common patterns expose the gap:

- We delay forgiveness until emotions change.
- We justify holding on because it feels deserved.
- We avoid reconciliation because it is uncomfortable.
- We maintain distance while calling it wisdom.

The problem is not that we are not unable to forgive. The problem is that we are unwilling to release it. The significant issue is that we say we have forgiven, but in reality we continue to keep the record. We say we have forgiven but continue to rehearse what happened. We move forward externally but carry the burden internally. We will stop talking about an offense while still holding onto it.

The real issue is resistance to letting go.

4. HOW TO PRAY DIFFERENTLY

When forgiveness is incomplete, your prayers reveal it. You pray:

- "Help me move on."
- "Fix this relationship."
- "Change them."

These prayers focus on resolution, but avoid responsibility:

- "Help me release this offense fully."
- "Show me where I am holding on."
- "Give me the willingness to take the first step."
- "Help me pursue peace, even when it is difficult."

Your prayers focus on external change instead of internal release. A prayer reset shifts from managing the situation to addressing your heart. Stop asking God to resolve the relationship, and ask Him to remove what is blocking it.

Forgiveness grows when prayer moves from justification to surrender. Unforgiven wounds will subtly shape your prayers and your relationships. If you are not willing to release the offense, the relationship will remain blocked.

Stop holding onto offense and start pursuing forgiveness and restoration.

5. TRANSFORMATIONAL PRAYER

Father, I confess that I do not always forgive as I should. I hold onto what has been done and resist letting it go. I hesitate to release the offense or take the first step to reconciliation.

Teach me to forgive fully. Help me to let go of what I have been holding onto and to stop rehearsing what has happened. Give me the ability to release the right to be justified.

Give me clarity on what steps I need to take toward reconciliation. I want the courage to act when it is appropriate. I surrender my desire to hold onto the offense. Replace it with a desire for peace and restoration.

Help me respond in a way that reflects Your forgiveness toward me.

6. SHORT ADDITIONAL PRAYERS

Help Me Release the Offense

Lord, give me the strength to let go of what I am holding onto.

Remove Resentment

Father, clear my thoughts from repeated focus on what has been done.

Give Me Courage to Act
Lord, help me take the first step toward reconciliation.

Guide My Response
Father, show me how to pursue peace with wisdom and clarity.

7. PERSONAL DIAGNOSTIC

1. What offense am I keeping alive by revisiting it?
2. Where have I said I have forgiven but continue to hold onto it?
3. What relationship am I avoiding instead of addressing?
4. What am I avoiding because reconciliation would require humility or active engagement?

When offense is revisited or avoided rather than addressed, it remains active and shapes how you see the other person. This reveals a pattern of withholding forgiveness while maintaining the appearance of resolution.

What is not released continues to influence your responses and keeps reconciliation out of reach. Avoidance does not remove the issue; it preserves it. What you hold onto continues to hold onto you.

Identify the offense you have not fully released and address it directly. This will not resolve until you release it. Decide what you will forgive and take the step toward reconciliation now.

My response:

I will ____________________________.

8. REAL-LIFE INTEGRATION

Forgiveness and reconciliation are practiced in ongoing choices:

- In whether you replay or release the offense.
- In whether you allow distance to build up.
- Letting go of the right to hold someone's wrong against them.
- Refusing to allow resentment to shape your thinking.
- Taking steps toward restoration when appropriate.
- Seeking peace without compromising truth.

These decisions form patterns. What you pray about the situation will shape how you respond. If your prayers focus on justification for the offense, you will hold on. If your prayers focus on release, your heart and actions will begin to change.

Forgiveness does not occur once; rather it is maintained through repeated decisions to forgive.

9. TAKE THIS STEP TODAY

Identify one unresolved offense or strained relationship. This week:

- Acknowledge the offense honestly in prayer.
- Make a clear decision to release it.
- Take one step toward peace (even if small).

Focus on your responsibility, not the outcome.

10. FINAL DECLARATION

I will forgive and quickly pursue restored relationships.

Chapter 15
PRAYING FOR SPIRITUAL GROWTH

Prayers of Eternal Significance – Spiritual Maturity in Others

1. REFRAME THE PRIORITY

We pray for people's circumstances but not for their spiritual growth. It is right to focus on visible needs such as health, protection, or outcomes. These are important but they are not eternal in nature. A person's spiritual condition (their growth in faith and maturity) has far greater and lasting significance.

Prayers of eternal significance should be prayed for the spiritual growth of others. If we consistently prioritize temporary or worldly concerns over spiritual development, we will miss what matters most.

2. WHAT THIS LOOKS LIKE

Praying for spiritual growth focuses on maturity, obedience, and relationship with God. It means praying for:

- A deeper understanding of God's truth.
- A growing desire to obey Him.
- Strength to resist sin and temptation.
- Consistency in spiritual disciplines.
- Increased faith during difficulty.
- Alignment between belief and behavior.

This kind of prayer looks beyond immediate needs and focuses on long-term transformation. It is not vague and must be specific and intentional. You are asking God to shape who they are becoming.

3. EXPOSE THE GAP

Most believers pray for others but in limited ways. Common patterns reveal the gap:

- Prayers focus on physical or situational needs.
- Requests are general rather than specific.
- Spiritual growth is assumed rather than intentionally laid before God.
- Prayer is reactive instead of consistent and ongoing.

We are not failing to pray, but are simply prioritizing the wrong things. The deeper issue is that we pray for relief, but overlook what God may be building. We do not prioritize or understand what God is doing in their life through their present circumstances.

It is possible to pray regularly for someone and rarely pray for what really matters most in their spiritual life. The issue is usually not that we don't pray, it's what we pray for.

4. HOW TO PRAY DIFFERENTLY

When your focus is limited your prayers reflect it:

- "Help them through this."
- "Provide what they need."
- "Fix the situation."

These are valid but incomplete. You rarely pray:

- "Grow their faith through this situation."
- "Strengthen their obedience in this area."
- "Help them respond in a way that honors You."
- "Develop their character through what they face."

Prayer often becomes centered on relief rather than spiritual growth. A prayer reset shifts from temporary outcomes to eternal development. Instead of praying "make this easier for them," pray "use this to grow them."

This does not ignore their needs, but prioritizes what lasts. If you never pray for someone's spiritual growth, you may be doing them a great disservice. If you only pray for improved circumstances, you may be missing what God is doing internally in their life.

Stop focusing on external needs and start praying for the spiritual maturity of others.

5. TRANSFORMATIONAL PRAYER

Father, I confess that I pray for others in ways that focus on their immediate needs rather than their spiritual growth.

Teach me to pray with a different focus. Help me to see beyond circumstances and prioritize their faith, obedience, and maturity. Show me how to pray specifically for their relationship with You.

Give them clarity where they are uncertain. Help them respond to challenges in ways that reflect trust and obedience in You. Develop their spiritual character through what they are facing.

Align my prayers with what should matter most and support their spiritual growth in ways that are lasting and meaningful.

6. SHORT ADDITIONAL PRAYERS

Strengthen Their Faith
Lord, deepen their trust in You, especially in difficult times.

Grow Their Obedience
Father, help them respond to You with faithfulness.

Develop Their Character
Lord, use their situation to shape who they are becoming.

Give Them Understanding
Father, help them see what You are teaching them.

7. PERSONAL DIAGNOSTIC

1. What do my prayers reveal I value most in others?
2. How often do I intentionally pray for someone's spiritual growth?
3. Do my prayers reflect eternal priorities or are they worldly concerns?
4. Where am I choosing relief over spiritual growth?
5. What am I avoiding by not praying more specifically for their spiritual life?

When prayers focus on relief or external outcomes, spiritual growth becomes secondary and often neglected. This shapes how you see people, limiting your concern to their immediate needs rather than lasting maturity. It reveals a pattern of valuing what is visible over what is eternal.

What you pray for will influence what you pursue for others. What you pray for determines what you seek in others. If this does not change, their growth will remain limited.

Decide how you will begin praying for spiritual maturity and make it specific. My response:

I will ______________________________.

8. REAL-LIFE INTEGRATION

Praying for spiritual growth changes how you view others.

- You begin to see beyond their circumstances.
- You become more attentive to their spiritual needs.
- Your conversations become more purposeful.
- Your encouragement becomes more focused.

This shift affects both prayer and action. What you consistently pray for will shape what you notice and how you respond to them. If you pray for growth, you will begin to recognize where it is needed and how to support it.

9. TAKE THIS STEP TODAY

Choose one person for whom you regularly pray. For the next seven days:

- Pray specifically for one aspect of their spiritual growth each day.
- Keep your focus on that one person and that one area.

Be clear, consistent, and intentional.

10. FINAL DECLARATION

I will pray for spiritual growth and the obedience of others.

Chapter 16
SERVING ONE ANOTHER

Prayers of Eternal Significance – Selfless Action

1. REFRAME THE PRIORITY

We value serving others, but prefer convenience and enjoy personal recognition. Service is widely accepted as part of the Christian life, yet the motivation behind it is often mixed. We serve when it fits our schedule, when it aligns with our preferences, or when it is noticed. When it becomes costly or inconvenient, we hesitate.

Prayers focused on eternal significance must confront this seriously. True service is defined by humility. It is measured by the posture and purpose behind it. If humility is absent, your help will become selective and self-serving.

2. WHAT THIS LOOKS LIKE

Serving one another humbly is the only desire when acting for the benefit of others. It is buoyed by putting others first and not seeking personal advantage. It includes:

- humility as a posture.
- internal motives.
- the concept of serving others before self.

3. EXPOSE THE GAP

Most believers serve, but not consistently or humbly. Common patterns reveal the gap:

- We serve when it fits our schedule, but hesitate when it disrupts it.
- We prefer roles that are visible or appreciated.
- We become frustrated when efforts go unnoticed.
- We avoid opportunities that feel small, inconvenient, or uncomfortable.

We are not unwilling to serve, but are simply selective in how we serve. The deeper issue is that we are willing to serve only until it does not cost us something. We choose when, where, and how we serve. We gravitate toward what aligns with our preferences and avoid what stretches us. Such service is filtered through comfort rather than shaped by humility.

4. HOW TO PRAY DIFFERENTLY

When your serving is selective, your prayers will reflect it. You pray, "use me" or "help me serve." These are good but incomplete. You don't pray:

- "Help me serve when it is inconvenient."
- "Remove my need for being recognized."
- "Give me the ability to do what I would avoid."
- "Shape my motives so I serve for the right reasons."

Our prayer tends to focus on activity instead of transformation. A prayer reset means we shift from a willingness to serve to serving humbly. You may have to stop praying "give me opportunities" and rather pray "change how I respond to the opportunities I already have."

Humble service evolves when prayer moves from preference to surrender. It begins where recognition is no longer an issue. If you require attention, your involvement will remain limited.

Stop seeking recognition in serving and start meeting needs with humility.

5. TRANSFORMATIONAL PRAYER

Father, I confess that my help is not always given in humility. I am willing to help, but I choose what is convenient or comfortable. I look for recognition, even if I do not say it openly.

Teach me to serve with humility. Show me where my motives are shaped by personal preference. Give me the willingness to serve in ways that are unseen or inconvenient. Help me respond to needs without filtering them through my own priorities.

I surrender my desire for recognition and control to You. Shape my heart so that my works reflect humility and not self-interest. Use my service to benefit others in ways that are genuine and lasting.

6. SHORT ADDITIONAL PRAYERS

Shape My Motives
Lord, align my heart so I serve for the right reasons.

Remove My Need for Recognition
Father, help me to act without desiring acknowledgment.

Make Me Willing to Serve Anywhere
Lord, give me readiness to help in any situation.

Strengthen My Consistency
Father, help me serve steadily, not only when it is convenient.

7. PERSONAL DIAGNOSTIC

1. What service do I avoid because it will costs me?
2. Do I choose serving based on preference or need?
3. How do I respond when my efforts go unnoticed?
4. Where am I avoiding being involved because it is inconvenient?

5. Why am I serving? What are my motives?

When serving depends on visibility or convenience, humility is replaced by self-interest, even if the action appears helpful. You are avoiding the cost of meeting real needs.

What you seek through serving will determine how and when you engage. Service that centers on you will remain selective and inconsistent. Your service reveals what you are willing to give without return.

Identify where you are avoiding humble service and address it directly. Decide where you will serve without recognition and follow through consistently.

My response:

I will ______________________________.

8. REAL-LIFE INTEGRATION

Serving others means:

- Choosing to help even when it is inconvenient.
- Taking action without needing acknowledgment.
- Prioritizing others' needs above personal comfort.
- Doing what is needed, not just what is preferred.
- Remaining willing to serve in unseen ways.

Humble service is about posture and priority. You place the needs of others ahead of yourself. It is seen in whether you serve consistently or selectively. These are not isolated moments but they begin to form patterns of humble service over time.

What you pray about serving will shape how you act. If your prayers focus on opportunity, you may remain selective. If your prayers focus on humility, your response will begin to change. True Christian service is defined by humility, consistency, and selflessness.

9. TAKE THIS STEP TODAY

Each day this week, choose one act that is intentional and unseen.

- Do something helpful for someone without drawing attention to it.
- Do not mention it afterward.
- Do not expect acknowledgment.

Keep your focus on the action, not the response.

10. FINAL DECLARATION

I will serve others humbly without seeking recognition.

Chapter 17
SPEAKING TRUTH IN LOVE

Prayers of Eternal Significance – Honest Accountability

1. REFRAME THE PRIORITY

We choose between truth and love, but our approach must include both. Some avoid hard conversations to preserve peace. Others speak directly but without care for how it is received. In both cases, something is missing. Truth without love becomes harsh, and love without truth is incomplete.

Eternally significant prayers address this balance. Growth in others requires honesty shaped by humility. When honesty and integrity are withheld or delivered poorly, relationships and spiritual maturity can both be affected.

2. WHAT THIS LOOKS LIKE

Speaking truth is the intentional act of communicating what is true in a way that is constructive and motivated by affection. It means:

- balanced communication, and
- communicating truthfully in love.

This does not mean being silent to avoid discomfort. It does not justify harshness as being honest. It is honest communication shaped by humility and purpose. This is not always easy because it requires thought and intentionality.

3. EXPOSE THE GAP

Most believers recognize the need but struggle to accomplish it. Typical patterns reveal the gap:

- We avoid difficult conversations to maintain comfort.
- We delay addressing issues until they grow.
- We speak indirectly rather than clearly.
- We become blunt when frustrated.

In this environment you are not lacking awareness; rather you are avoiding discomfort. Silence often feels easier than speaking. Directness feels risky. You delay, soften, or avoid a conversation. This allows problems to grow.

It is also possible to speak truth without love. You can use the excuse of honesty to express frustration rather than to build up or encourage. Something is being avoided: either the discomfort of speaking or the need to speak with love.

4. HOW TO PRAY DIFFERENTLY

When your communication is misaligned, your prayers reveal it. You pray "help them understand" or "fix this situation." These prayers focus on outcome, but avoid preparation.
We rarely pray:

- "Help me speak clearly and wisely."
- "Shape my tone and timing."
- "Give me the courage to say what needs to be said."
- "Help me speak in a way that builds, not damages."

Effective communication requires intentional preparation. A prayer reset shifts from hoping the conversation goes well to preparing for it. Stop praying "make this easier," and instead pray "make me faithful in how I speak."

Truth delivered well requires thought and restraint. These are strengthened through prayer. If you do not plan how you will speak, you will either not respond or react poorly.

Stop avoiding the truth and speak with integrity, love, and responsibility.

5. TRANSFORMATIONAL PRAYER

> Father, I confess that I do not always speak with integrity. I avoid difficult conversations when I should speak. Other times I speak too quickly or too directly without considering how my words will affect others.
>
> Teach me to communicate with clarity. Help me choose words that build up, not tear down. Guide my timing and my tone. Help me prepare before I speak, not react in a moment of stress.
>
> I surrender my desire for comfort and my tendency toward reaction. Shape my words so they reflect both truth and love.

6. SHORT ADDITIONAL PRAYERS

Give Me Courage to Speak
Lord, help me address what truly needs to be said and do it without hesitation.

Guide My Words
Father, shape my communication so it constructive.

Control My Tone
Lord, help me speak with patience.

Prepare My Heart
Father, align my intentions before I speak to others.

7. PERSONAL DIAGNOSTIC

1. What truth am I avoiding because it is uncomfortable?
2. When do I either avoid speaking or speak without appropriate filters?
3. How do I respond when I feel frustrated or pressured?
4. Where am I choosing comfort over clarity?

5. What am I avoiding because speaking honestly would require courage or restraint?

When truth is avoided or delivered without care, communication becomes ineffective and relationships weaken. This creates a pattern where necessary conversations are postponed or handled poorly, allowing issues to persist.

What is left unspoken or is spoken carelessly will not produce the intended result. Truth must be spoken to be effective.

Identify the situation where truth is being avoided and address it directly. If this does not happen, the issue will remain unresolved. Decide how you will communicate clearly and act on it now.

My response:

I will ______________________________.

8. REAL-LIFE INTEGRATION

Speaking with love means you prepare and deliver your words with gentleness and care.

- Saying what needs to be said, not delaying it.
- Speaking with clarity but never exaggeration.
- Choosing words that are intended to help.
- Addressing issues directly rather than indirectly.
- Remaining committed to the person.

Speaking truth is practiced in specific moments when you notice something that needs to be addressed. It means speaking even when you feel the tension between silence and honesty, knowing your words can either build up or damage.

These moments require careful consideration, not reaction. What you pray about will shape how you respond. If you pray for clarity and control, your words will start to become more measured and effective. Remember, communication is not neutral, it either strengthens or weakens.

9. TAKE THIS STEP TODAY

Identify one conversation you have been avoiding. This week:

- Pray specifically for clarity, timing, and tone.
- Plan what needs to be said in advance.
- Take one step toward having that conversation.

Do not delay once you are prepared.

10. FINAL DECLARATION

I will speak truth with love, courage, and responsibility.

Chapter 18
STRENGTHENING THE CHURCH

Prayers of Eternal Significance – Health and Mission

1. REFRAME THE PRIORITY

Many of us think about our own spiritual growth but give little or no attention to the health of the church as a whole. Our focus should be on personal faith and relationships. Yet Scripture consistently points beyond the individual to the body, the church as a unified and mission-focused community. When the church is weak, its impact is limited regardless of the effort of individual followers.

Eternally significant prayers must expand beyond the individual. What you pray about the church reflects whether you see yourself as part of the faith community, or not

2. WHAT THIS LOOKS LIKE

Strengthening the church focuses on its health and mission. It means you should be praying for:

- Unity among members despite differences.
- Spiritual maturity across the congregation.
- Faithful and wise leadership.
- Clear teaching and sound doctrine.
- Active participation and shared responsibility.
- A focused commitment to missions.

3. EXPOSE THE GAP

Most believers care about their church but do not consistently pray for it. Common patterns reveal the gap:

- Prayer is focused on personal needs, not the church.

- The concerns about believers are discussed more than prayed about.
- Frustrations are observed but not addressed spiritually.
- Involvement is limited and responsibility is minimized.

This does not mean you are disconnected, but you may be disengaged. The deeper problem is that you critique or complain about people or leaders while contributing little to a solution. You notice what is lacking, identify what could improve, and then stop there. You observe instead of engage.

You can attend regularly and still contribute little to the strength and vitality of the church. The problem becomes limited ownership.

4. HOW TO PRAY DIFFERENTLY

When your focus is limited to individuals, your prayers reflect it. You pray for your own needs, for people you know personally, and for situations that affect you directly.
You rarely pray:

- "Strengthen the unity of our fellowship."
- "Guide and protect our leaders."
- "Deepen the spiritual maturity of our congregation."
- "Align our faith community with Your mission."

The church becomes under-supported in prayer. A prayer reset shifts your focus from personal concerns to the whole body. Stop praying only "help me grow," and instead pray "strengthen the body I am part of."

This does not replace personal prayer. It expands it. The strength of the church grows when individuals pray for issues and success beyond themselves. A weak fellowship is the result of shallow prayer. If you do not pray for the church, you will remain disconnected from its purpose.

Stop thinking only about individual needs and start praying for the health and mission of the whole body.

5. TRANSFORMATIONAL PRAYER

Father, I confess that I focus on my own needs and growth without giving consistent attention to the health of the church. I notice issues or areas that could improve, but I do not always bring them to You in prayer.

Teach me to see my faith community differently. Help me recognize that I am part of a larger fellowship and that its health matters. Strengthen relationships within the fellowship so that unity is preserved. Guide our leader's wisdom and clarity.

I surrender my passive approach and my tendency to observe without engaging. Align my perspective with what matters for the health and strength of the entire body.

6. SHORT ADDITIONAL PRAYERS

Strengthen Our Unity
Lord, help our church remain unified despite differences.

Guide Our Leaders
Father, give wisdom and clarity to those who lead.

Grow Our Maturity
Lord, help each follower grow spiritually in their faith.

Align Us with Your Mission
Father, keep our focus on what You have called us to do.

7. PERSONAL DIAGNOSTIC

1. Do I pray for the church as often as I evaluate it?
2. Do I focus more on what is lacking, or on supporting what is needed?
3. Where am I choosing passivity over responsibility?

4. How do I respond when I see problems? Do I engage or withdraw?
5. What am I avoiding by not praying for the church?

When your prayer is limited to personal needs, responsibility for the whole is reduced and engagement becomes passive. This produces a consistent cycle in which problems are observed but not addressed. The result is the health of the church is left to others.

What you do not invest in will not be strengthened. What you do not support will remain weak. Passive concern does not build anything. Identify where you have withdrawn from responsibility and address it directly.

If this does not change, your impact will remain minimal. Decide how you will actively support the church in prayer and follow through consistently.

My response:

I will ______________________________.

8. REAL-LIFE INTEGRATION

This is not an abstract concern. It is specific and practical. It is seen in:

- How people relate and speak to one another.
- How leadership functions.
- How the faith community engages its mission.

You are responsible for its strength and resilience to some measure. Strengthening the church is revealed in how you speak about the people and whether you support or criticize them. Are you taking responsibility for your role?

These patterns shape the overall health of the faith community. What you pray about the church will influence how you act within it. If your prayers are limited, your involvement will be limited. When your prayers expand, your perspective and actions will follow.

9. TAKE THIS STEP TODAY

For the next seven days, set aside time each day to pray specifically for your church. Focus on:

- One aspect of its health (unity, leadership, maturity, or mission)
- One group within your faith community (leaders, members, or specific ministries)

Be intentional and consistent.

10. FINAL DECLARATION

I will pray for the strength, unity, and mission of the church.

Part 3 - Prayers For the World

Engaging those beyond the Church

This section has one purpose: to move your prayers beyond your life and into God's larger environment.

You can stay focused on what you can see: your responsibilities, your relationships and your immediate concerns. But God's purposes extend far beyond that. He is working in lives, communities, cultures, and nations. Prayer is one of the ways you participate in that work.

If your prayers never move beyond your immediate locale, your perspective will shrink. When your perspective shrinks, your engagement will as well. You were not meant to live at that level.

Prayer expands your awareness, but it also defines your participation. What you consistently pray for shapes what you notice and respond to.

Remember, if your prayers never move beyond you, your life will remain centered on yourself. What you are centered on must reach what God intends.

Expand your focus and engage an expanded world.

Chapter 19
SALVATION OF THE LOST

Prayers of Eternal Significance – People Coming to Christ

1. REFRAME THE PRIORITY

We may care about people and their wellbeing but overlook their eternity. The most significant reality in any person's life is their relationship with God. Everything else is temporary in comparison to eternity.

Your prayer life should reflect this priority. If the eternal condition of people is not consistently in view, prayer becomes centered on what is immediate rather than on what matters most. You pray for what you truly value.

2. WHAT THIS LOOKS LIKE

Praying for the lost is centered on their response and reaction to the Gospel of Christ. You should pray for the lost to come to know Christ personally and respond to Him in faith. That means praying for:

- Open hearts to recognize truth.
- Clarity in understanding the message of the Gospel.
- Conviction of sin and their need for a Savior.
- Willingness to respond in faith.
- Removal of barriers that prevent belief.
- Opportunities for them to hear and respond.

This is not vague concern, but a specific and purposeful undertaking. It looks beyond behavior or circumstances and focuses on their relationship with God. You are asking God to transform their spiritual condition.

3. EXPOSE THE GAP

Most believers care about others, but do not consistently pray for their salvation. Prayer patterns reveal the gap:

- Prayer concentrates on worldly needs not eternity.
- Concern remains internal rather than expressed in prayer.
- Opportunities to pray for specific individuals are overlooked.
- Fear or hesitation limits intentional prayer.

This does not necessarily mean you are indifferent, but you may be unfocused. You live around people who are spiritually lost, but rarely carry that burden into your prayer life. You may interact and share life, but you do not consistently bring their spiritual condition before God. Urgency fades and your concern becomes passive.

You may care deeply and still neglect this need. The problem is that you lack sustained focus.

4. HOW TO PRAY DIFFERENTLY

When eternity is not prioritized, your prayers reflect it. You pray "help them," "bless them," or "take care of them." These are not wrong, but they are not enough. We must shift from simply hoping people come to Christ to praying with intention that they do. You rarely pray:

- "Open their heart to truth."
- "Help them see their need for You."
- "Give them clarity and understanding."
- "Position me to speak when the opportunity comes."

A prayer reset will shift your prayer from broad concern to specific intercession. Stop saying "be with them," but instead pray "draw them to Yourself." Praying for salvation requires consistency and being intentionally centered on salvation. If you do not pray for the lost, urgency fades, and intent is lost. You will soon lose interest in their plight.

Stop overlooking the lost and start praying urgently for their salvation.

5. TRANSFORMATIONAL PRAYER

Father, I confess that I live among people who do not know You and I do not consistently pray for them. Teach me to pray with clarity and purpose. Help me see people as You see them and recognize their need for You. Give me a deeper concern that moves me to consistent prayer.

Open their hearts to understand truth. Remove barriers that keep them from responding. Help them see their need for You and give them a deep desire to know Christ.

Position me to speak when I have the opportunity. I surrender my hesitation and distraction.

6. SHORT ADDITIONAL PRAYERS

Open Their Heart
Lord, help them recognize truth and respond to it.

Give Them Clarity
Father, remove confusion and help them know who You are.

Draw Them to Yourself
Lord, create a desire in them to seek and respond to You.

Use Me Faithfully
Father, help me recognize and respond to opportunities to share my faith.

7. PERSONAL DIAGNOSTIC

1. What am I avoiding by not focusing on the lost and their spiritual condition?
2. How often do I intentionally pray for their salvation?
3. Am I concerned about their eternity or only personal worldly matters?
4. What keeps me from praying consistently for them?
5. Who have I overlooked that I should be praying for?

Your answers reveal who you recognize as spiritually lost and whether that recognition shapes your prayers. When eternity is acknowledged but not acted upon, urgency fades and concern remains passive. This creates a pattern in which relationships are maintained while the spiritual reality is ignored.

What you do not consistently bring before God will not be central in your thinking. This is not lack of awareness, but rather lack of intentional response. If you do not act, nothing about their direction will change through you.

Identify the person whom you know is not following Christ and bring their condition into focus. Decide who you will begin praying for consistently and act on it without delay.

My response:

I will ______________________________.

8. REAL-LIFE INTEGRATION

Praying for the lost affects how you live:

- You become more aware of spiritual conversations.
- You listen more carefully to what people say.
- You recognize opportunities that would be missed.
- You engage with greater purpose.

Praying changes both your perspective and your response. What you consistently pray about will shape what you notice.

If you pray for the lost, you will begin to see opportunities to have gospel conversations. If you do not, those moments will pass unnoticed.

9. TAKE THIS STEP TODAY

Identify one specific person who does not know Christ. For the next seven days:

- Pray for that person by name each day.
- Focus on one clear request related to their salvation.
- Remain attentive for opportunities to engage.

Keep your prayer specific and consistent.

10. FINAL DECLARATION

I will pray consistently for the salvation of those who do not know Christ.

Chapter 20
BOLDNESS AND THE GOSPEL

Prayers of Eternal Significance – Living and Speaking with Courage

1. REFRAME THE PRIORITY

Most prayers related to the gospel focus on outcomes. People ask for others to be saved, hearts to change, and the message of Christ to spread. These are necessary prayers. But there is another important part that is often neglected.

God works through people and creates opportunities for the gospel to be seen and heard. He wants disciples to step into those moments with clarity and courage.

This means prayer is not only about asking God to move. It is about asking God to prepare you to become involved when He moves.

2. WHAT THIS LOOKS LIKE

Praying for boldness and opportunity begins with awareness of what God is doing. You can recognize that God is already at work around you. He will be creating conversations, opening doors, and placing people in your path.

Instead of viewing these moments as interruptions, you should see them as invitations. You should be attentive to what God is doing and willing to respond when the opportunity presents itself.

This kind of prayer also reshapes your response to fear. Rather than avoiding situations that feel uncomfortable, you begin to face them with a growing confidence that God will give you what you need in the moment. Your focus shifts from your ability to His power.

When you pray, you become involved and are more available and responsive. You are not forcing opportunities, but you are no longer missing them.

3. EXPOSE THE GAP

You can care about the gospel without actively participating in it. Many believers pray for others to come to Christ, yet remain silent when opportunities arise to share their faith. The danger is that you just become inactive.

Fear is often the explanation because it produces concern over rejection or discomfort. You are afraid you may say the wrong thing. But beneath that is the deeper issue of separating belief from action.

There can also be a pattern of passivity. Opportunities are missed because either they are not recognized or not acted upon. Life becomes busy, conversations stay surface-level, and the opportunity passes.

You may think prayer alone is enough. But when prayer is not joined with participation, it becomes incomplete.

4. HOW TO PRAY DIFFERENTLY

Ask God to make you aware of the opportunities He is already providing. Pray for sensitivity to recognize when a conversation can go deeper, when a question opens a door, or when someone is ready to hear the truth.

Ask for boldness that is not forced. You are not trying to manufacture confidence, but wanting God's presence in the moment. Pray for the willingness to speak clearly, even when it feels uncomfortable.

Ask for readiness. Pray that your words would be thoughtful, timely, and guided by truth. Remember, you are not responsible for the outcome; you are only responsible for delivering the message.

This kind of prayer will move you from passive agreement to active participation. You are no longer simply waiting for ideal conditions. You are asking God to prepare you to act when the moment comes. If you are not prepared to respond, you will continue to miss what God is doing.

Stop remaining passive about the gospel and start praying for the opportunities God provides.

5. TRANSFORMATIONAL PRAYER

> Father, I know that You are at work in the lives of people around me, yet I often fail to recognize the opportunities You place before me. Too often I have remained silent when I should have spoken.
>
> Make me aware of what You are doing. Open my eyes to see the opportunities. And then give me the willingness and courage to respond.
>
> Remove the fear that holds me back. Help me to trust that You will be present with me and that You will guide my words when I step forward in obedience. Prepare my heart and mind so that I am ready when the moment comes.
>
> I do not want to remain passive. I want to participate in what You are doing. I want to speak with courage when You give me the opportunity.

6. SHORT ADDITIONAL PRAYERS

Help Me Truly See
Help me recognize the opportunities You provide.

Give Me Courage
Give me courage to speak when the moment comes.

Help Me Speak Clearly
Guide my words with clarity and truth.

Keep Me Alert To The Needs
Keep me attentive to what You are doing around me.

7. PERSONAL DIAGNOSTIC

1. When opportunities arise, do I step up or stay silent?
2. What fears stop me from speaking?
3. Am I aware of the opportunities or am I distracted?
4. Does my prayer life prepare me or keep me passive?
5. What opportunity have I recently missed?

When hesitation or fear takes over, moments are lost and lives remain unchanged. This creates a pattern where awareness exists, but response does not follow.

What you do not engage will be missed, and repeated inaction will create your pattern. This is not about your ability; it's about your willingness in the moment.

Identify any opportunity you avoided or delayed and address it directly. If you do not act, the moment is lost. Decide how you will respond the next time opportunity appears and follow through immediately.

My response:

I will ______________________________.

8. REAL-LIFE INTEGRATION

This kind of prayer changes how you move through everyday gospel interactions. Conversations are no longer only about exchanging information, but become opportunities to listen more closely and respond more intentionally.

You begin to notice when someone is searching, struggling, or asking deeper questions. Instead of avoiding those moments, you engage them with clarity and gentleness. You do not try to control the conversation, but you are willing to guide it when the opportunity arises.

It also changes your expectations. You are no longer waiting for ideal or dramatic situations. You recognize that small ordinary moments can have great significance.

Over time, your life becomes more aligned with God's mission. Not because you are forcing activity, but because you are responding when He provides opportunities.

9. TAKE THIS STEP TODAY

Identify one person in your life where there may be an opportunity for a deeper conversation. Pray specifically for awareness and boldness and to be prepared to take one important step toward that conversation the next time the opportunity occurs.

10. FINAL DECLARATION

I will recognize the opportunities God gives me and respond with truth and courage.

Chapter 21
PRAYING FOR LEADERS

Prayers of Eternal Significance – Wisdom and Justice

1. REFRAME THE PRIORITY

We react to leaders, but rarely do we pray for them with consistency. Leadership decisions affect the lives and stability of many. Yet most responses to leadership are impacted by opinion, agreement, or frustration rather than intentional prayer. It is easier to complain than to pray.

A prayer life focused on what matters includes praying for leaders. They influence outcomes far beyond what we can see. If we are not praying for them, we are left to engage at the level of reaction.

2. WHAT THIS LOOKS LIKE

Praying for leaders and authorities is the intentional focus on their wisdom, character, decisions, and alignment with what is right. It means praying for:

- Wisdom in decision-making.
- Integrity in leadership.
- Justice in actions and policies.
- Clarity in judgment.
- Restraint from harmful choices.
- Alignment with truth and righteousness.

This applies to all those in authority: government, organizations, church, or any position of authority that influences others. This is not passive praying: it is directed and purposeful. You are not just responding to the leadership of others, rather you are asking God to influence their judgment and actions.

3. EXPOSE THE GAP

Most believers think or complain about authorities, but do not consistently pray for them. The common response is:

- We discuss leadership decisions more than we pray about them.
- We focus on agreement or disagreement rather than on intercession.
- We pray only when situations affect us directly.
- We allow frustration to replace responsibility.

The danger can be that you become disengaged, instead of interceding regularly. The problem occurs when you only react to leaders instead of supporting them through prayer. You evaluate and form opinions, but do not consistently bring those concerns before God.

Over time, your response is shaped by reaction to their decisions instead of intercession. You may have strong opinions about leadership, but offer little meaningful support through prayer. The problem is misplaced engagement.

4. HOW TO PRAY DIFFERENTLY

When your response is reactive, your prayers will be "fix this situation" or "change what is happening." These are outcome-focused, but incomplete. You don't pray:

- "Give them wisdom in this decision."
- "Shape their thinking toward what is right."
- "Restrain what would cause harm."
- "Strengthen their integrity under pressure."

Your prayers are not asking for transformation. A prayer reset shifts from *reacting* to *interceding* for those making decisions. Stop praying "change the outcome" and instead pray "help this leader make the right choices." Although this is more difficult, it is more effective.

Prayer moves from what is typically surface-level frustration to deeper influence. The one praying changes from simply reacting to leadership to influencing it through prayer. Prayer will shape how you engage with leadership and how you respond to their policies. If reacting to leadership is all you do, you will never influence it through prayer.

Stop criticizing leadership without prayer and start asking God to guide them with understanding and wisdom.

5. TRANSFORMATIONAL PRAYER

Father, I confess that I often respond to authorities with either agreement or frustration. Seldom do I pray for them. I do not always bring my concerns before You with clarity and purpose.

Teach me to pray differently. Help me focus not only on what is happening, but on those who are responsible for leading. Grant them wisdom in their decisions. Strengthen their integrity when they are under pressure.

Restrain choices that would cause harm and position them to act with clarity and fairness.

I surrender my tendency to react without praying. Use my prayers to influence leadership that aligns with Your plans.

6. SHORT ADDITIONAL PRAYERS

Give Them Wisdom

Lord, guide their thinking so they make sound decisions.

Strengthen Their Integrity
Father, help them act with honesty and justice.

Direct Their Judgment
Lord, lead them toward what is right.

Restrain Harmful Decisions
Father, prevent actions that would cause unnecessary harm.

7. PERSONAL DIAGNOSTIC

1. Do I pray for leaders as often as I think about them?
2. Do I respond with opinion or with intercession?
3. When I disagree do I pray, or do I only talk about it?
4. Where have I allowed frustration to replace duty?
5. What am I avoiding by reacting instead of praying?

When your attention is directed toward opinion rather than prayer, influence is replaced with commentary. This establishes a recurring tendency in which frustration grows while responsibility is avoided. What you consistently think about without praying over will shape your attitude without producing change. This is not a lack of concern but a misplaced response.

What you respond to in prayer will shape your influence. If you do not pray, your response will remain ineffective. Decide how you will begin praying consistently for leadership and act on it now. Who do you need to be praying for?

My response:

I will ______________________________.

8. REAL-LIFE INTEGRATION

Praying for authorities affects how you engage with leadership.

- You become less reactive and more intentional.

- Your perspective shifts from criticism to responsibility.
- You recognize the weight of decisions others carry.
- You respond with clarity rather than frustration.

These perspectives impact how you think and respond. What you pray about leadership will shape how you speak about it. If you pray consistently, your response will become more measured and purposeful.

Leadership is influenced by the prayers of those affected by them.

9. TAKE THIS STEP TODAY

Identify one leader you know or are aware of. For the next seven days:

- Pray for that person by name each day.
- Focus on one area: wisdom, integrity, or judgment.
- Keep your prayers specific and consistent.

Do not shift your focus and stay intentional.

10. FINAL DECLARATION

I will pray for leaders to act with wisdom, justice, and righteousness.

Chapter 22
JUSTICE IN SOCIETY

Prayers of Eternal Significance – Moral Alignment

1. REFRAME THE PRIORITY

You talk about what is wrong more than you pray for what is needed. Recognizing injustice or moral confusion is often easy. These issues are visible and openly discussed. Yet recognizing them is not the same as addressing them. Without intentional prayer, awareness becomes commentary instead of contribution.

A prayer life concerned about eternal significance must move beyond observation. Justice and righteousness are not sustained by simple awareness. They require alignment with God's standards and must be exercised at levels we do not control. You must pray for alignment with what is right to influence the power source.

2. WHAT THIS LOOKS LIKE

Praying for justice and righteousness in society is the intentional focus on moral alignment with God in decisions and behavior across a broader culture. It means praying for:

- Truth to be recognized and upheld.
- Justice to be applied fairly and consistently.
- Leaders to act with integrity and restraint.
- Cultural systems reflect what is right rather than what is expedient.
- Exposure and correction of what is unjust.

This is not a theoretical problem. It is specific and requires attention. It involves cultural patterns, institutional decisions, and individual choices. Instead of simply reacting to what is wrong; you are asking God to establish what is right.

3. EXPOSE THE GAP

Most believers recognize the problems but do not pray for alignment. Common prayer patterns include:

- discussing issues more than interceding for them.
- reacting emotionally rather than being intentional.
- focusing on outcomes without addressing the underlying causes.
- becoming discouraged rather than engaged.

You may often react instead of interceding. You are quick to identify what is wrong, but slow to bring it before God. You form opinions, follow developments, and respond to events, but you do not consistently translate that awareness into focused prayer. As time passes concern becomes just reaction, not responsibility.

You are typically informed about injustice, but not engaged in addressing it through prayer. The underlying problem is a lack of sustained intercession.

4. HOW TO PRAY DIFFERENTLY

When your response is reactive, your prayer will reflect it. You will pray "fix what is happening" or "change the situation" or even "stop what is wrong." These are understandable but not adequate. You are not praying to:

- Establish what is right at every level.
- Align decisions with truth and justice.
- Expose what is hidden and correct it.
- Strengthen those who are acting with integrity.

Your prayers focus on stopping problems instead of establishing alignment. You need to reset your prayer focus from reacting to what is wrong to asking for what is right to be established. Stop praying "remove this issue" and instead pray "establish what is right."

This moves your prayer to a focus on foundational influences. A society drifts and ultimately fails when righteousness is no longer valued. If you are not praying for what is right, you will simply react and pray for what is wrong.

Stop accepting moral compromise and start praying for alignment with God's standards.

5. TRANSFORMATIONAL PRAYER

Father, I confess that I often respond to issues in society only with awareness or frustration, and not with consistent and intentional prayer. I see what is wrong, but I do not bring it before You with clarity and purpose.

Teach me to pray differently. Help me to focus on what must be established. Align my thinking with what is true and right, not just what is visible. Establish justice where there is injustice. Expose what is hidden and correct what is wrong.

Strengthen those who act with righteousness. Restrain actions that would cause harm or injustice. I surrender my tendency to react without engaging.

6. SHORT ADDITIONAL PRAYERS

Establish What Is Right
Lord, bring alignment with truth in decisions and actions.

Expose What Is Hidden
Father, reveal injustice and bring correction.

Strengthen Integrity
Lord, support those who act with honesty and courage.

Restrain Harm
Father, prevent actions that would lead to further injustice.

7. PERSONAL DIAGNOSTIC

1. Do I pray about societal issues like I discuss them?
2. Do I react to problems or intercede for solutions?
3. What issues have I noticed but not prayed about?
4. Where has frustration replaced intentional prayer?
5. What am I avoiding by staying informed but not being engaged in prayer?

Your answers expose how you engage with what is wrong around you. When awareness leads to frustration but not intercession, concern becomes passive and produces no real solutions. This reveals a pattern of observing problems without taking the responsibility to address them in prayer.

What you consistently notice but do not act on will remain unchanged. Reaction without intercession leaves issues unresolved. Identify the issue you recognize but have not consistently prayed about and address it specifically. Decide what you will begin praying consistently and follow through.

My response:

I will ______________________________.

8. REAL-LIFE INTEGRATION

Praying for justice and righteousness changes how you engage with society:

- You move from reaction to responsibility.
- Your thinking becomes measured and intentional.
- You respond with clarity rather than impulse.

- You maintain focus on what is right.
- You consider a broader spectrum of issues.

This reshapes both perspective and behavior. What you consistently pray about will shape how you respond. If you do not pray, reaction will dominate your responses. When you pray with clarity, your thinking and engagement will become more purposeful.

Lasting change begins at the level of understanding God's will and ways (alignment) about what's right.

9. TAKE THIS STEP TODAY

Identify one specific issue or area of concern in society. For the next seven days:

- Pray daily for that issue with one clear focus.
- Keep your prayer specific and consistent.
- Avoid shifting topics, stay engaged with one focus.

Consistency matters more than variety.

10. FINAL DECLARATION

I will pray for society to align with God's standards.

Chapter 23
COMPASSION FOR THE NEEDY

Prayers of Eternal Significance – Care for the Vulnerable

1. REFRAME THE PRIORITY

You notice people in need, but you just don't consistently respond to it. Seeing need is easy because the realities are visible in both distant places and everyday life. But awareness does not necessarily produce action.

Prayers rooted in eternal significance must address this because compassion is revealed by how you respond. It is not measured by emotion or feelings. If need is consistently observed but rarely carried into the prayer room your concern will be passive.

2. WHAT THIS LOOKS LIKE

Compassion for the needy is the intentional choice to recognize suffering and respond with both prayer and practical concern. It means:

- Noticing those who are overlooked or vulnerable.
- Allowing their situation to affect both your thinking and response.
- Praying specifically for their needs and circumstances.
- Refusing to ignore or minimize visible need.

This means purposeful engagement. It requires awareness, prayer, and a willingness to engage. You need to recognize suffering and have a response.

3. EXPOSE THE GAP

Most people recognize need, but do not struggle with it. The gap can be described as:

- We notice need but move on quickly.
- We assume others will respond.
- We feel concern but do not translate it into action.
- We avoid situations that require involvement.

The fact is you are not unaware. You are just not engaged. Exposure reduces urgency instead of increasing responsibility and repeated exposure often reduces response. The more you see, the easier it becomes to look away. You become accustomed to what should move you. Concern fades into familiarity and familiarity will reduce both your concern and participation.

You can be aware of suffering and remain largely unaffected. The issue is a refusal to engage. This can be caused by either apathy or fear, but the end result is a loss of engagement.

4. HOW TO PRAY DIFFERENTLY

When your response is limited, your prayers will be vague and unfocussed: "help and provide for those in need." This is a reasonable prayer but inadequate. You need to be praying:

- "Help me respond when I see need."
- "Make me attentive instead of indifferent."
- "Show me where I can act."
- "Keep my concern from fading into inaction."

If this is not how you pray, your prayer will remain broad and your response will be limited. You need a prayer reset that shifts from general awareness to personal responsibility. You cannot pray "take care of them." Instead you must pray "use me where I am able."

Compassion grows when prayer moves from distant concern to engaged response. Compassion for others that is ignored in prayer rarely produces interest in providing real help. If you are not willing to engage, your compassion remains distant and ineffective, regardless of what you think or say.

Stop overlooking the vulnerable and start remembering them with genuine compassion.

5. TRANSFORMATIONAL PRAYER

Father, I confess that I often see need but do not respond as I should. I feel concern in the moment, but I do not carry it into consistent prayer or action.

Teach me to respond. Help me remain attentive to those who are overlooked or struggling. I do not want to be indifferent or distant. Show me where I can respond in simple and practical ways. Help me pray effectively.

Remove my tendency to assume others will respond. I surrender my inaction. Use me to reflect compassion in ways that are real and meaningful.

6. SHORT ADDITIONAL PRAYERS

Make Me Attentive
Lord, help me notice need and not ignore it.

Keep Me Engaged
Father, prevent my concern from fading into inaction.

Show Me Where to Act
Lord, guide me toward practical ways to respond.

Strengthen My Consistency
Father, help me remain committed beyond the moment.

7. PERSONAL DIAGNOSTIC

1. How do I actually respond when I see need?
2. Do I move on quickly or stay engaged in prayer?
3. Where have I assumed others would respond instead of becoming involved?
4. What situations do I avoid because they require my involvement?
5. What am I choosing not to see because responding would require commitment?

When prayer or engagement is brief or avoided, compassion becomes selective and does not lead to sustained care. This exposes a pattern of recognizing need without allowing it to impact your response.

Compassion is measured by active response, not simply awareness. What you pass over quickly will not remain a priority. Compassion that does not lead to action is incomplete.

Identify where you have chosen distance instead of involvement and address it directly. If you do not engage, nothing will change through you. Decide where you will remain involved and act on it consistently.

My response:

I will ______________________________.

8. REAL-LIFE INTEGRATION

Compassion means being willing to act, not just observe. You maintain concern over time, not just in the moment. You practice compassion by responding.

Compassion is revealed in everyday situations, like:

- noticing those who are overlooked.

- responding when something could be done.
- remaining engaged beyond the initial moment.
- choosing to act instead of moving on.

Opportunities are frequently missed. What you pray about shapes how you respond. When your prayers remain general, your compassion will be limited. When your prayers become specific, your awareness and response will increase. Compassion is sustained by continual engagement.

9. TAKE THIS STEP TODAY

Identify one specific need you have recently observed.
This week:

- Pray for that situation daily with one clear request.
- Take one simple action if it is within your ability.
- Do not delay once the opportunity is clear.
- Do not wait for a better opportunity. Act on the one you already see.

Keep your response focused and consistent.

10. FINAL DECLARATION

I will remember and pray for those who are suffering.

Chapter 24
STABILITY IN THE WORLD

Prayers of Eternal Significance – Conditions for Godly Living

1. REFRAME THE PRIORITY

We desire peace for our personal comfort but often overlook its purpose. We want safety and calm conditions. Yet peace is not only about comfort. It creates the conditions for something greater. Without stability our focus is scattered, and what matters most is often delayed or neglected.

A prayer life built around eternal significance must recognize the need for peace and stability, but they are not the end goal. They are the conditions that make everything else possible. If we desire peace only for personal ease, we miss its broader purpose.

2. WHAT THIS LOOKS LIKE

Praying for peace and stability in the world is intentionally focusing on conditions that allow people to live, grow, and respond to God without unnecessary disruption or chaos. It means praying for:

- Reduction of conflict.
- Order in systems and societies.
- Protection from widespread disruption.
- Conditions that allow daily life to function.
- Space for truth to be heard and practiced.
- Environments where faith can be lived out openly.

This is focused and purposeful because contentment creates opportunity, clarity, and continuity. You are not simply asking for calm; you are asking for conditions that allow what is right to take place.

3. EXPOSE THE GAP

Most people desire calm and the lack of chaos, but they do not consistently pray for it. Typical patterns reveal the gap:

- We react to chaos rather than intercede for stability.
- We focus on immediate disruption instead of the underlying conditions.
- We believe peace is normal until it is removed.
- We think in terms of personal impact rather than broader societal need.

The truth is you are being reactive. The deeper issue is you value peace when it is disrupted, but rarely pursue it before it is lost. Most of us become aware of instability only when it affects us. Until then, it remains unaddressed in prayer.

This creates a reactive pattern rather than a consistent one. We all benefit from stability but few of us support it through prayer. The issue becomes a significant lack of attention.

4. HOW TO PRAY DIFFERENTLY

When peace is taken for granted you pray:

- "Help this situation."
- "Bring resolution."
- "Restore what has been disrupted."

These are reactive and situation-specific. You rarely pray:

- "Sustain conditions that allow peace and stability."
- "Prevent disruption before it begins."
- "Establish order where there is potential for chaos."
- "Protect environments in which people can live and respond to You."

Your prayers react to disruption rather than supporting stability beforehand. A prayer reset is required. A prayer reset shifts your prayers from reacting to stress and chaos to sustaining conditions for stability. Stop praying "fix what is happening." Rather, pray "preserve what allows life and faith to function."

Peace is not only restored but is maintained through intentional prayer. If you pray only when stability is lost, you will never support what sustains it.

Stop taking stability for granted and start praying for conditions that allow godly living to flourish.

5. TRANSFORMATIONAL PRAYER

Father, I confess that I often take peace for granted. I notice disruption when it happens, but I do not consistently pray for the conditions that prevent it.

Teach me to pray with a wider perspective that allows others to live, grow, and respond to You. Establish peace where there is potential for conflict. Maintain order where disruption could arise.

Guide leaders and systems so they support stability rather than undermine it. Help me to pray consistently for what sustains life and faith, not just what restores it.

6. SHORT ADDITIONAL PRAYERS

Establish Stability
Lord, create conditions where life functions with order and contentment.

Prevent Disruption
Father, restrain forces that would lead to conflict.

Sustain Peace
Lord, maintain environments where people can live and grow.

Protect Opportunity
Father, preserve conditions where truth is heard and practiced.

7. PERSONAL DIAGNOSTIC

1. Do I pray for peace before life is disrupted?
2. Do I pray to prevent disruption or simply react when it happens?
3. Where have I taken stability for granted?
4. Do I think about how a peaceful life affects others?
5. Do I pray for conditions to sustain peaceful existence?

Do you value stability enough to pray for it before it is disrupted? When peace is assumed rather than pursued, it becomes invisible until it is lost. This creates an ongoing sequence in which you react to instability instead of praying in advance for the conditions that allow life to function and faith to grow.

What is taken for granted is rarely protected. Stability will not remain steady independently without consistent prayer. Identify where you have assumed peace without interceding for it.

Conditions shape how life is lived. Decide what conditions you will begin praying for consistently and act on it now.

My response:

I will ____________________________.

8. REAL-LIFE INTEGRATION

Praying for peace and stability shapes how you engage with the world.

- You become more aware of what supports daily life.
- You recognize the value of order and continuity.
- You respond with clarity instead of reaction.
- You maintain focus on what allows peace and stability.

What you consistently pray about shapes how you think. If you pray only during disruption, your response will be reactive. If you pray consistently for peace and stability, your awareness and engagement will become more grounded.

9. TAKE THIS STEP TODAY

For the next seven days, begin each day with one focused request. Pray specifically for peace, security, or stability in one area of your life or the world. Keep your focus consistent for the full week. Consistency strengthens your awareness.

10. FINAL DECLARATION

I will pray for peace and stability that allows godly living.

Chapter 25
SPIRITUAL AWAKENING

Prayers of Eternal Significance – Mass Returning to God

1. REFRAME THE PRIORITY

We desire change in the world but overlook the need for changing the hearts of men and women around us. We focus on external conditions or visible problems. These are usually measurable and immediate. Yet lasting transformation does not begin at the surface. It begins when individuals turn back to God with conviction.

Revival is not primarily about improved conditions. It is first about restored alignment with God. Spiritual awakening is marked by a return to what has been spiritually neglected. We cannot be concerned about this while ignoring prayers for revival and spiritual awakening.

2. WHAT THIS LOOKS LIKE

Revival and spiritual awakening are focused on the widespread return to God. It occurs when individuals and communities realign their lives with truth, conviction, and obedience to God. This means we should be praying for:

- Awareness of spiritual condition.
- Conviction that leads to genuine change.
- Desire to return to what is right.
- Clarity about truth and error.
- Willingness to turn from apathy.
- Renewed commitment to obedience.

This is not about emotional intensity. It's about directional change. It involves both individuals and broader communities.

You are praying for lasting realignment with the one true God of the universe.

3. EXPOSE THE GAP

Most believers desire revival, but do not consistently pray for it:

- We speak about the need for change but do not intercede for it.
- We focus on external problems rather than personal internal alignment with God.
- We expect change to come through activity rather than spiritual transformation.
- We treat revival as an event rather than a process.
- We want revival for others, but avoid it personally.

The typical believer is disengaged from the process. The issue is that you want visible change around you but avoid the necessary spiritual change required. You look for improvement in others while overlooking our own need for realignment. This creates distance between what you desire and what you pursue.

You can talk about revival and even deeply desire it but remain largely unaffected because there is no personal spiritual response. The need is for personal engagement at a level that produces transformation.

4. HOW TO PRAY DIFFERENTLY

When your focus is external, your prayers reflect it. You pray "bring revival" or "move in a powerful way." But these are broad and undefined requests. Instead pray:

- "Begin realignment in me."
- "Expose what is out of place in my life."
- "Lead others to recognize and respond to truth."
- "Create sustained change, not temporary response."

Your prayers remain general instead of specific. A prayer reset shifts from asking for large-scale change to engaging personally with the process of realignment. Stop praying "send revival" and begin praying "let it begin with me."

Revival cannot be requested from a distance. It must be pursued through consistent, focused, personal prayer for transformation. If you are not personally engaged, revival will remain an idea rather than a reality. Revival begins when prayer becomes honest and persistent.

Stop expecting change without engagement and start praying for the widespread return to God.

5. TRANSFORMATIONAL PRAYER

Father, I confess that I often desire change around me without consistently pursuing change within me. I do not always engage in prayer that supports realignment in a meaningful way.

Begin with me. Show me where I am misaligned, passive, or where I have accepted what should be corrected. Give me clarity to see spiritual truth and the willingness to respond to it.

Lead others to recognize their need for change. Create conviction that leads to realignment, not just awareness. Use my prayers to support genuine awakening that begins with me and extends outward through my church and my community.

6. SHORT ADDITIONAL PRAYERS

Begin With Me
Lord, expose what needs to change in my life.

Create Conviction
Father, bring clarity that leads to realignment.

Awaken Awareness
Lord, help others recognize their need to return to God.

Establish Lasting Change
Father, create transformation that does not fade.

7. PERSONAL DIAGNOSTIC

1. Do I desire revival more than I pursue it?
2. Where have I expected change in others without addressing my own condition?
3. What areas of my life remain unchanged?
4. Do I pray specifically for transformation, or only in generic terms?
5. What am I avoiding by keeping revival at a distance?

These questions reveal whether your desire for change extends beyond observation. When revival is desired without personal alignment, it remains distant and undefined. This exposes a desire for transformation in others while avoiding the necessary response within yourself.

What you keep at a distance will not shape you, and what does not shape you will not happen through you. Broad desire without specific response produces no real change. Revival begins where alignment is real.

Identify the area in your life that remains unchanged and address it directly. If this does not change *in* you, it will not change *through* you. Decide what changes you will address personally and act on it now.

My response:

I will ______________________________.

8. REAL-LIFE INTEGRATION

Revival begins by specific and consistent responses:

- In recognizing where change is needed.
- In responding when conviction is present.
- In maintaining alignment.
- In influencing others through clarity and engagement.

These are not large moments, they are repeated decisions. What you pray about revival will shape how you live. If your prayers remain broad and universal, your response will be limited. As your prayers become more specific, your awareness and engagement will deepen. Revival is sustained by consistent alignment with spiritual values.

9. TAKE THIS STEP TODAY

For the next seven days, focus on one area of personal alignment:

- Identify one area that needs correction or strengthening.
- Pray specifically for that area each day.
- Take one clear action that reflects change.
- Stay with the same issue all week.

Keep your focus narrow and consistent.

10. FINAL DECLARATION

I will pray for hearts to turn back to God.

Chapter 26
PROTECTION FROM EVIL

Prayers of Eternal Significance – Restraint of Darkness

1. REFRAME THE PRIORITY

We ask for personal protection from trouble but rarely consider the broader influence and presence of evil. We pray for personal safety and protection in our own lives. Yet wickedness is not limited to individual experience. It operates at wider levels, influencing decisions, systems, and communities that affect many people and places.

Prayers of eternal significance must recognize both the existence and the presence of evil. Protection is a personal concept and global in scope. If we pray only for ourselves, we overlook the need for intervention at levels far beyond our immediate view.

2. WHAT THIS LOOKS LIKE

Praying against evil in the world intentionally focuses on restraining and limiting the evil forces that impact both individuals and society as a whole. It means praying for:

- Restraint of harmful actions and intentions.
- Exposure of hidden wrongdoing.
- Protection of the vulnerable.
- Limitation on influence that leads to suffering.
- Clarity to recognize what is wrong.
- Strength for people to resist and reject sin.

This is not an abstract or theoretical concept. It is real and must be targeted. It involves personal choices, organizational actions, structures, and cultural patterns. You are praying not only for protection but are asking for evil to be restrained where it would otherwise advance.

3. EXPOSE THE GAP

Most people recognize the presence of evil, but do not consistently pray about it. Prayer patterns reveal the gap:

- You respond to visible events but ignore the underlying influence.
- You focus on outcomes rather than causes.
- You pray for safety but not for restraint of what causes harm.
- You avoid thinking about the scope of the problem.

You address symptoms instead of causes. You address what you can see while ignoring what causes it. You react to events and consequences, but do not consistently bring the broader influence of evil before God. This limits your prayer engagement to surface-level issues. The problem becomes your limited scope in prayer.

4. HOW TO PRAY DIFFERENTLY

When your focus is narrow, your prayers reflect it. The prayer shift that is necessary requires asking for safety from what creates the danger. You pray "keep me safe" or "protect my family." These are appropriate, but not adequate. It would be more effective to pray:

- "Restrain evil where it is forming."
- "Expose what is hidden before it causes harm."
- "Limit influence that leads to destruction."
- "Strengthen people to resist what is evil."

This is a significant problem because if your prayers remain personal, local, and limited, the problem expands. Your prayers must reset and shift from individual protection to include broader restraint. Expand praying "protect me from harm" to pray "limit what produces harm." This changes your prayer from being self-focused to purpose-driven.

Being safe and secure is not just about avoidance. It is about intervention at the source. Sinful behavior grows when it is not resisted or prayed against. If you pray only for safety, you are ignoring what actually produces the threat.

Stop ignoring the presence of evil and start praying for its restraint and for spiritual protection.

5. TRANSFORMATIONAL PRAYER

> Father, I confess that I often limit my prayers for protection to my own life and circumstances. I do not consistently pray for the restraint of the evil that causes sin and suffering.
>
> Help me to recognize that evil operates beyond what I can see and that my prayers should reflect and address that reality.
>
> Restrain harmful actions before they are carried out. Expose what is hidden before it causes damage. Limit influence that leads people toward what is wrong. Protect those who are vulnerable and strengthen those who are resisting.

6. SHORT ADDITIONAL PRAYERS

Restrain Sin and Evil
Lord, limit actions and intentions that would cause damage.

Expose What Is Hidden
Father, bring wrongdoing into the light before it spreads.

Protect the Vulnerable
Lord, guard those who are at risk or vulnerable.

Strengthen Resistance
Father, help people stand firm against wickedness and evil.

7. PERSONAL DIAGNOSTIC

1. Do I pray for my own protection rather than the broader restraint of evil?
2. Do I pray about causes or only outcomes?
3. Where have I ignored the larger scope of that which produces harm?
4. Do I avoid thinking about this because it feels beyond my control?
5. What am I neglecting by keeping my prayers focused only on my own safety?

Your responses show how narrowly or broadly you understand what needs to be addressed. When prayer remains focused on personal safety, the larger forces that produce or support evil are left unchallenged. You are responding to outcomes rather than recognizing and interceding for what produces them.

What is not addressed at its source will continue to produce the same results. Expanding your perspective changes how you pray and what you expect. Scope determines effectiveness. If you do not widen your focus, your impact remains limited.

Identify where your focus has been limited and correct it intentionally. Decide what you will begin praying about that is beyond yourself and follow through consistently.

My response:

I will ______________________________.

8. REAL-LIFE INTEGRATION

Praying for protection from evil determines how you engage with the world.

- You become more aware of underlying influences.
- You think beyond immediate outcomes.
- You respond with greater clarity and purpose.
- You recognize the importance of restraint.

This reshapes both thinking and response. What you pray about will shape how you respond. If your prayers remain personal, your perspective will remain narrow. If your prayers expand, your awareness and engagement will deepen.

9. TAKE THIS STEP TODAY

For the next seven days, expand your focus intentionally:

- Each day, include one prayer for the restraint of evil.
- Choose one area (e.g. community, leadership, culture) and remain consistent.
- Keep your request specific and focused.

Your consistency will strengthen clarity.

10. FINAL DECLARATION

I will pray for the restraint of evil and for spiritual protection.

PART 4 – PRAYERS FOR YOUR LIFE

Align Yourself With God's Ways

This section has one purpose: to bring your life into alignment with what you have been praying.

You began with God. You extended your focus to others and then the world. Now you can return to your own life with greater clarity and responsibility.

The focus is no longer your circumstances. It is your character, your obedience, and your direction. This is where real change can take place.

You tend to pray for relief from circumstances. Few consistently pray for transformation. As we have repeated constantly, what you consistently pray for will shape what your life becomes. Prayer is not only about what you ask; it is also about establishing and forming your life.

Your life follows the direction of your prayers. If your prayers do not change, neither will your life.

So choose your direction and alignment carefully. Pray with intention and focus on areas of eternal significance.

Chapter 27
WISDOM AND GOD'S WILL

Prayers of Eternal Significance – Choosing Alignment with God

1. REFRAME THE PRIORITY

You pray for clarity when facing decisions. You want to know what to do, which path to take, or how things will turn out. The focus is often on outcomes: making the right choice, avoiding mistakes, and securing a good result. But in addition to getting answers, prayer must be about alignment.

The real issue is not whether you are making a good decision. It is whether your thinking and direction are being shaped by God. Without that alignment, even a well-informed decision can move you away from what matters most.

Prayers of eternal significance are not just about finding the easiest or safest path. They are also about becoming the kind of person who recognizes and chooses what honors God.

2. WHAT THIS LOOKS LIKE

Praying for wisdom and God's will begin with a shift in your posture. Instead of asking God to confirm your preferences, you begin by asking Him to shape them. You are not simply seeking direction, but are seeking transformation in how you think and decide.

This means slowing down your instincts and submitting your reasoning to God. It means allowing His truth not your emotions or circumstances to define what takes priority. What once seemed desirable will lose its appeal, and what seemed difficult will become the obvious path.

This kind of prayer produces clarity, but not always in the way you expect. It clarifies what matters rather than what is easy. It reshapes your priorities before it directs your steps.

3. EXPOSE THE GAP

Most prayers for guidance are centered on outcomes. The concern is usually "What decision will work best for me?" or "What will lead to the result I want?" Even when God is included, the underlying goal often remains unchanged, which creates a significant problem.

You may be asking God for direction while still holding onto control. You want His input, but you retain your authority on how to proceed. You want direction without surrender. When something seems reasonable or beneficial, you quickly assume is right. Prayer becomes a formality rather than a genuine surrender of decision-making.

The result is a pattern in which your decisions are made first and then brought to God for approval, instead of being shaped by Him.

4. HOW TO PRAY THIS DIFFERENTLY

Begin by asking God to align your thinking before you ask Him to direct your choices. Make it your aim to think in alignment with His truth, not simply to arrive at your preferred outcome. Ask Him to reveal your motives, expose your assumptions, and correct anything that is not consistent with His will.

Pray for the ability to recognize what is right. Ask for clarity about what honors Him, even if it requires sacrifice or discomfort. Instead of asking for immediate answers, ask for a heart that is willing to follow wherever He leads.

This kind of prayer changes how you live your life! You are no longer asking God to confirm your direction. You are inviting Him to define it.

Stop relying on your own judgment and start seeking God's wisdom and direction as the foundation for every decision.

5. TRANSFORMATIONAL PRAYER

Father, I come to You knowing that my understanding is limited and often shaped by my own desires. I have made decisions based on what seems right to me, and not asked for Your guidance. I have not given up control.

Change the way I think. Help me to see clearly what honors You and to recognize what leads me away from Your purposes. Align my desires with Your will. Where I resist Your direction, give me the willingness and courage to follow.

Teach me to trust You fully, even when the path is not clear. I do not want to simply make good decisions. I want to make decisions that reflect Your will and bring You glory.

6. SHORT PRAYERS FOR THIS

Help Me Choose
Give me wisdom to see clearly and choose rightly.

Align My Thinking
Align my thinking with Your truth.

Help Me Honor You
Show me what honors You in this decision.

Give Me Trust
Help me trust Your direction over my understanding.

7. PERSONAL DIAGNOSTIC

1. When I face decisions, do I seek God's will or confirmation of my own decisions?
2. What does my recent decision-making reveal about who I truly trust?
3. Where am I relying on my own judgment instead of seeking God's wisdom?
4. Am I willing to follow God's direction even if it leads away from what I want?
5. What decisions have I made without seeking God's direction?

These questions reveal how you approach decisions. When judgment is formed before seeking God's direction, outcomes reflect your own preferences rather than alignment with His ways. This creates a pattern in which decisions feel right but lack true spiritual guidance.

What you decide without seeking God will reflect your personal preferences and understanding. You are making a choice not to seek His wisdom. Direction follows what you trust. If you rely on yourself, your path will reflect it.

Identify decisions you have already made without seeking God and address them directly. Decide where you will seek God's direction and act on it before moving forward.

My response:

I will ____________________________.

8. REAL-LIFE INTEGRATION

This kind of prayer changes how you approach everyday decisions. Instead of reacting quickly, you begin to pause and consider what aligns with His truth. You weigh options differently; not just by outcomes, but by what reflects His character and priorities.

It also affects how you handle uncertainty. When the path is unclear, you are not driven by anxiety to force a decision. You remain steady, praying and trusting that God is shaping your thinking as much as He is guiding your steps.

As you follow His lead, your decisions become more consistent. Not because every situation is easy, but because your foundation has changed. You are no longer guided by impulse or personal preference, but by a growing alignment with God.

9. TAKE THIS STEP TODAY

Identify one decision you are currently facing. Before making a choice, set aside time to pray specifically for wisdom and alignment. Write down what you believe honors God in that situation. Then commit to following that direction, even if it is not the easiest option.

10. FINAL DECLARATION

I will seek God's wisdom and align my decisions with His ways.

Chapter 28
CONFESSION AND REPENTANCE

Prayers of Eternal Significance – Cleansing and Humility

1. REFRAME THE PRIORITY

You seek and pray for spiritual growth but never consider what prevents growth from occurring. It is common to pray for strength and improvement. Yet unresolved sin quietly limits progress. What is left unaddressed continues to shape and impact your thinking and decisions.

This is not a minor issue because unaddressed sin limits meaningful progress. Confession and repentance are not occasional practices, but ongoing requirements for alignment with God's ways. Without them, clarity fades, conviction dulls, and progress becomes inconsistent.

2. WHAT THIS LOOKS LIKE

Confession and repentance are the acts of recognizing and turning from what is wrong. It means:

- Identifying attitudes and actions that are not right.
- Acknowledging them without minimizing them.
- Admitting responsibility without shifting blame.
- Turning away from what is wrong.
- Seeking alignment rather than relief from discomfort.
- Maintaining a posture of humility, not defensiveness.

Confession and repentance are concrete and unavoidable issues that a disciple must address. It involves thought patterns, choices, habits, and our responses to conviction. The issue is not about the existence of sin or how to manage guilt, but the restoration of alignment with God.

3. EXPOSE THE GAP

Repentance is meant to be a continuous process. Ignoring that process is revealed when:

- We speak broadly rather than being specific.
- We feel regret but do not change direction.
- We delay addressing what we already recognize as sin.
- We minimize what requires correction.

The deeper issue is you prefer to feel better rather than align with what is right. You may acknowledge something is wrong, but stop short of addressing it specifically. This leads to a recurring outcome in which awareness increases, but change does not follow.

What once would have prompted a corrective response becomes tolerated. You recognize what is wrong without fully addressing it. You may even confess the problem but still allow it to remain unchanged.

4. HOW TO PRAY DIFFERENTLY

When confession is incomplete, your prayers reflect it. You may pray "forgive me" or "help me do better." You may even ask for cleansing. These are sincere but vague. You rarely pray:

- "This is where I was wrong."
- "This is what needs to change."
- "Remove my tendency to return to this pattern."
- "Strengthen my resolve to turn from it fully."

In practice your prayers seek relief instead of change. This is where your prayer must shift and reset your focus. It must move from general admission to specific alignment.

Stop praying "forgive my sins" but instead pray "this is the exact issue I am addressing and I need help." Clarity produces change. Vagueness maintains existing habits and patterns. When your confession becomes specific, transformation becomes possible. If you are not being specific in prayer, you will remain unchanged in practice.

Stop minimizing sin and start responding with honest confession and repentance.

5. TRANSFORMATIONAL PRAYER

Father, I confess that I acknowledge sin in general terms without addressing it clearly. I recognize something is wrong, but I delay, minimize, or move past it quickly.

Show me where I am misaligned in my thinking, choices, and actions. Give me the clarity to see it fully and the honesty to admit it without excuse.

Remove my tendency to justify or delay. Strengthen my willingness to turn from what is wrong, not just feel regret about it. Help me to follow through with real change.

I surrender my resistance. Do not allow me to remain unchanged where correction is needed.

6. SHORT ADDITIONAL PRAYERS

Show Me Clearly
Lord, reveal clearly what I need to address in my life.

Make Me Honest
Father, give me the courage to admit what is wrong.

Strengthen My Resolve
Lord, help me turn fully from what I know is sinful.

Keep Me Responsive
Father, prevent me from ignoring what requires correction.

7. PERSONAL DIAGNOSTIC

1. What sin have I recognized but not addressed clearly?
2. Where do I speak in general terms instead of naming what is really wrong?
3. Where have I delayed response after conviction?
4. What patterns have I allowed to continue without making corrections?
5. What am I avoiding by keeping my confession vague?

Your answers expose behavior that you have recognized but not addressed. When sin is left unnamed or your response is delayed, it remains active and continues to shape your life. This reveals a pattern of allowing what is known to persist without correction. What is not confessed will not be fixed or removed.

Avoidance does not lessen its effect; it allows it to continue. Identify the specific sin you have not addressed and bring it into full clarity. If this is not addressed, it will continue. Decide what you will confess and act on it without delay.

My response:

I will ______________________________.

8. REAL-LIFE INTEGRATION

Confession and repentance must be practiced in real time:

- When conviction is recognized.
- When a wrong choice is identified.
- When a pattern becomes clear.
- When correction is required immediately.

These are not necessarily rare moments. They may occur frequently but are ignored. If they are not addressed in prayer, they will continue to be a stumbling block. If your prayers remain general, your habits will remain unchanged. If your prayers become more specific, your actions will begin to reflect change. Alignment is maintained through consistent prayer and intentional correction.

9. TAKE THIS STEP TODAY

For the next seven days:

At the end of each day, identify one specific area that needs correction. Name it clearly in one sentence. Then, pray one direct request for change. Determine one adjustment for the next day.

Do this at the same time each day.

10. FINAL DECLARATION

I will confess my sin honestly and turn from it quickly.

Chapter 29
HOLINESS AND PURITY

Prayers of Eternal Significance – Freedom From Sin

1. REFRAME THE PRIORITY

You desire spiritual growth, but tolerate what prevents it. You pray for spiritual growth but accept what continues to undermine it. You want to move forward and live with purpose, but leave unaddressed what will eventually limit everything else: your holiness.

This is not a secondary issue. It affects everything else about your life. Holiness is about alignment with God at the deepest level. Purity can never be an optional refinement because it is the foundation for clarity, strength, and obedience.

2. WHAT THIS LOOKS LIKE

Holiness and purity are the intentional pursuit of freedom from sin and consistent alignment in thought, desire, and action with God's precepts and commands. It means:

- Rejecting what corrupts thinking or behavior.
- Maintaining clear boundaries rather than allowing gradual compromise.
- Choosing what is right even when it is not convenient.
- Guarding thought patterns as well as outward actions.
- Refusing to normalize what you know to be wrong.
- Acting with consistency in both private and public.

Holiness is more than simply avoiding wrongdoing. It is a mindset of pursuing consistent alignment with what God defines as "blameless."

3. EXPOSE THE GAP

Most people value purity in principle but allow accommodation in practice. Our actions reveal the gap:

- We tolerate small concessions while convincing ourselves they are insignificant.
- We justify behavior that does not align with what we know.
- We focus on visible actions while ignoring internal patterns and habits.
- We delay addressing what has already become a consistent or habitual problem.

You're probably not unaware of your weakness, you are simply allowing compromise. The issue is that you manage appearances to the outside world while allowing misalignment to continue in your inner being. You maintain a general sense of control while difficult areas remain unexamined.

This creates a chasm that can be difficult to overcome. The longer it continues, the easier it is to accept. The result is that you allow what you once rejected.

4. HOW TO PRAY DIFFERENTLY

When accommodation exists, it is not subtle. You pray:

- "Help me stay strong."
- "Keep me from sin."
- "Give me discipline."

These are sincere but lack specificity. You need to pray:

- "Expose where I have not been steadfast."
- "Remove what I continue to tolerate."
- "Strengthen my resolve to reject what is wrong."
- "Make me consistent in private as well as public."

Your prayer must become a tool for change, not a way to avoid it. It must shift from resisting failure after it occurs to eliminating compromise in order to prevent damage. Stop praying "help me avoid sin" and instead pray "remove every sin that I am allowing to remain." This is not about resisting sin. It is about removing what makes sin possible.

Holiness is not maintained by intention alone. It is sustained by consistent and specific correction. Purity begins where sin is not excused. If you tolerate accommodation, you will continue to return to it.

Stop tolerating sin and start pursuing a life set apart for God.

5. TRANSFORMATIONAL PRAYER

Father, I confess that I allow compromise to remain in small ways. I recognize what is wrong, but I tolerate it, delay addressing it, or minimize its impact on my life.

Show me clearly where I am misaligned. Expose habits I have accepted and behaviors I have justified. Help me to see the full effect of what I have allowed to rule in my life.

Give me the resolve to reject what is wrong immediately, not gradually. Strengthen my willingness to act with consistency in both private and public areas of my life.

Create a pattern of clarity and correction. Do not allow me to continue in what I know should be removed. Make my response decisive.

6. SHORT ADDITIONAL PRAYERS

Expose Compromise
Lord, reveal any sin I have allowed to remain and remove it.

Strengthen My Resolve
Father, help me act immediately when something is not right.

Guard My Thinking
Lord, keep my thoughts aligned and free from corruption.

Make Me Consistent
Father, align both my private and public life with Your ways.

7. PERSONAL DIAGNOSTIC

1. What specific compromise have I allowed to continue?
2. Where have I justified what I know is not right?
3. In what areas do I focus more on outward behavior than serious internal patterns?
4. What have I accepted that I would have once rejected?
5. What am I avoiding by not addressing this now?

Your answers reveal where compromise has been allowed to remain. When you tolerate or justify that which you already know to be wrong, it becomes normalized and gradually shapes your thinking and behavior. This allows it to continue without being corrected.

What is left unaddressed does not stay contained; it expands and influences other areas. Avoidance gives permission for continuation. Identify the specific compromise you have allowed and bring it into full clarity. If this is not addressed, it will continue to shape you. Decide what you will remove and act on it immediately.

My response:

I will ______________________________.

8. REAL-LIFE INTEGRATION

Holiness and purity are practiced in common daily decisions:

- In what you allow into your thinking.
- In how you respond when something is wrong.
- In what you choose to continue or eliminate.
- In whether you act immediately or delay.

These are not isolated moments; they are repeated choices. If holiness is not prayed for, challenges will remain before you. How you pray will shape how you respond.

If your prayers remain general, compromise will be easier and sin will continue to encircle your life. If your prayers become specific, your actions will become decisive. Holiness involves removing what should not remain at all.

Consistency in purity produces clarity in direction.

9. TAKE THIS STEP TODAY

For the next seven days:

- Identify one specific area of compromise.
- Name it clearly in one sentence.
- Remove or restrict it immediately where possible.
- Pray one direct request for consistency each day.

Do this at a specific time daily, even if it is brief. Do not adjust the focus; but stay with the same issue.

10. FINAL DECLARATION

I will pursue a life that is set apart and pleasing to God.

Chapter 30
OBEDIENCE AND FAITHFULNESS

Prayers of Eternal Significance – Doing What God Commands

1. REFRAME THE PRIORITY

You assess your spiritual growth by what you understand. What you understand will be demonstrated by your actions.

You can understand what is right and still fail to act on it. This creates a gap between belief and behavior that will weaken your life. Obedience is not simply an advanced step in the maturity process; it is the evidence that alignment is in place. Your faithfulness must be consistent because it is the foundation that defines your life!

This matters because life is not determined by intentions. Your life is demonstrated by your decisions and responses. What you repeatedly do shapes who you are.

2. WHAT THIS LOOKS LIKE

Obedience and faithfulness are the consistent practice of acting on what you know is right without delay, adjustment, or selective application. It means:

- Acting on clear direction rather than waiting for perfect or ideal conditions.
- Following through on your commitments.
- Choosing consistency over convenience.
- Responding immediately rather than postponing.
- Refusing to negotiate with what is clearly required.
- Maintaining steady attention even when there is no immediate result.

Obedience is not something you try or evaluate. Obedience is revealed in whether you act on what has been required.

3. EXPOSE THE GAP

A lack of obedience will appear in subtle ways:

- We wait for better timing before acting.
- We adjust what is required to fit our preferences.
- We act partially and consider it sufficient.
- We revisit decisions that were already clear.

The issue is not the lack of clarity. It is that you are postponing doing something. You may prefer agreement over taking action because agreement feels complete and does not actually require change. This creates a false sense of alignment. You believe you are moving forward because you understand or agree with something. But, change can't happen if you simply do nothing.

Delayed obedience is also dangerous because it trains you to resist what is clearly required. Selective obedience weakens alignment with what is right. Inconsistency weakens everything you do.

4. HOW TO PRAY DIFFERENTLY

When your obedience is inconsistent, your prayers become general, like "help me be faithful." These are sincere but incomplete and ineffective. Instead, pray:

- "Show me exactly where I am delaying action."
- "Remove my tendency to postpone what I know is right."
- "Strengthen my willingness to act immediately."
- "Hold me accountable for what I know is true."

The danger in simply asking for strength is lack of precision. What kind of strength are you asking for and for what? Instead of praying "help me obey more," begin praying "make me act immediately on what I already know." Obedience requires a decisive response to what is true. It is determined long before the moment of decision. If you put off what you know is right, you train yourself not to respond.

Stop delaying obedience and start doing exactly what God commands.

5. TRANSFORMATIONAL PRAYER

Father, I confess that I often postpone what I know I should do. I recognize what is right, but I hesitate, adjust, or postpone action.

Show me clearly where I am not acting on what I already understand. Expose patterns of delay and partial obedience. Do not allow me to remain comfortable with being inconsistent.

Give me the resolve to act immediately when direction is clear. Strengthen my willingness to follow through without adjustment or hesitation. Remove my tendency to revisit what has already been decided.

Establish a pattern of steady obedience and faithful follow-through in every area of my life.

6. SHORT ADDITIONAL PRAYERS

Act Without Delay
Lord, help me respond when I know what is right.

Strengthen My Follow-Through
Father, make me consistent in completing what I begin.

Remove My Hesitation
Lord, take away my tendency to postpone decisions.

Establish Faithfulness
Father, build a pattern of steady obedience in my life.

7. PERSONAL DIAGNOSTIC

1. What do I clearly know what to do but have not yet acted on?
2. Where am I postponing action under the appearance of wisdom or timing?
3. What commitment have I manipulated instead of fully completing?
4. Do I revisit decisions that were already clear?
5. What am I avoiding by not acting immediately?

Your answers show where clarity has not led to action. When decisions are delayed or revisited, obedience becomes inconsistent and loses its impact. This results in a tendency whereby what is known is adjusted or ignored instead of being pursued, creating conditional commitments.

What you postpone will not strengthen your direction; it will weaken it. This is not a situation in which you lack understanding. It is a refusal to act on what is already known.

Identify the action you have delayed and address it directly. If you do not act, nothing has changed. Decide what you will do and follow through without delay.

My response:

I will ______________________________.

8. REAL-LIFE INTEGRATION

Obedience and faithfulness are not occasional attributes, they are daily patterns:

- In how you respond when direction is clear.
- In whether you act immediately or postpone.
- In whether you complete what you begin.
- In whether you maintain consistency over time.

These are not large decisions considered alone. They are small repeated responses that occur daily. If obedience is not prayed for specifically, it will remain inconsistent. Your prayer habits impact your response patterns. If your prayers remain general or indecisive your obedience will be inconsistent. When your prayers become specific, your actions become decisive.

Faithfulness is built one consistent action at a time.

9. TAKE THIS STEP TODAY

For the next seven days:

- Identify one clear action you have delayed.
- Write it down in one sentence.
- Complete it within 24 hours.
- Do not adjust, postpone, or revisit it.

Each day, repeat this process with one action. Keep the focus narrow.

10. FINAL DECLARATION

I will obey God consistently and without delay.

Chapter 31
SPIRITUAL ENDURANCE

Prayers of Eternal Significance – Perseverance in Trials

1. REFRAME THE PRIORITY

Many people pray for relief from difficulty. Few pray for strength to endure it well. The instinct is understandable. Pressure and stress exposes weakness and creates uncertainty. But endurance is not about getting through a difficult time, it is about who you become while you are persevering.

Trials will test you and reveal what you rely on. If your endurance is strong, character will be formed. What you become under stress matters more than how quickly the pressure is overcome.

2. WHAT THIS LOOKS LIKE

Spiritual strength and resilience is the ability to remain steady, consistent, and aligned under pressure without abandoning spiritual principles. It includes:

- Continuing forward when progress feels slow. Maintaining clarity when life creates chaos.
- Acting consistently when emotions fluctuate.
- Keeping commitments when tension increases.
- Refusing to retreat into passivity or avoidance.
- Enduring without drifting or disengaging.

Perseverance is not proven at the beginning. It is revealed as time passes, challenges are endured, and strength is revealed.

3. EXPOSE THE GAP

You probably don't lack the desire to be steadfast, but persevering in difficult times can be a challenge. The endurance gap is evident in various ways:

- We start strong but fade when results are delayed.
- We look for alternatives when the process is difficult.
- We disengage quietly rather than stopping at once.
- We reduce our involvement while telling ourselves we are still committed.

You are not unwilling! The problem is you are inconsistent when the pressure increases. It's easy to assume something is wrong when it is difficult instead of recognizing difficulty as part of the process. This often leads to premature adjustment. Instead of staying the course, you look for relief, a change of direction, or even lowered expectations.

Resilience is never lost in a single moment. It erodes through small decisions to ease stress or back off gently. You do not remain steady or confront the issues.

4. HOW TO PRAY DIFFERENTLY

When perseverance is weak, your prayer often focuses on removing the distress. You will pray:

- "Take this situation away."
- "Make this easier."
- "Change the circumstances."
- "Give me relief from the stress."

These are natural but do not address the real underlying need:

- "Strengthen me to remain steady under pressure."
- "Build endurance when I want to withdraw."
- "Teach me to stay consistent when results are slow."
- "Develop strength in me through this trial so I will be stronger next time."

Your prayers may seek escape instead of change or transformation. Your prayer must shift from relief to strength. Stop praying "remove this difficulty" and instead pray "make me stronger within it." Endurance is not produced by avoiding tension. It's developed by remaining steady through it. Resilience is built up in prayer before it is required in life.

Stop depending on your strength and start relying on God to sustain you through trials.

5. TRANSFORMATIONAL PRAYER

Father, I confess that I often seek relief rather than enduring strength. I look for ways to ease the burden rather than remain steady within it.

Show me where I have allowed difficulty to weaken my commitment. Expose patterns of avoidance, silent disengagement, or reduced effort. Build perseverance in me where I withdraw. Teach me to continue with clarity and consistency even when progress is slow or unseen.

I surrender my desire for immediate relief. Form in me a steady strength that does not depend on current conditions. Establish endurance in me that will remain firm through every trial.

6. SHORT ADDITIONAL PRAYERS

Strength in Pressure
Lord, make me steady when circumstances become difficult.

Endurance Over Time
Father, help me remain consistent when results are delayed.

Clarity in Difficulty
Lord, keep my direction clear when tension creates confusion.

Resilience in Trials
Father, build strength in me that does not disappear when I am under stress.

7. PERSONAL DIAGNOSTIC

1. Where have I reduced my effort because progress felt slow?
2. What situations am I tempted to abandon?
3. Do I seek relief more quickly than being steadfast and pursuing endurance?
4. Where have I disengaged instead of being steadfast?
5. What forces am I avoiding that are forming poor habits and patterns in my life?

When engagement fades, endurance lags, and strength begins to decline. This creates a sequential pattern in which short-term relief is chosen over long-term resilience. The result is that growth is interrupted.

What you step away from will not develop and what you abandon will remain incomplete. This is an ineffective approach to difficult circumstances.

Identify where you have disengaged and address it directly. You are strengthened only by what you continue. Decide where you will remain steady and follow through consistently.

My response:

I will ______________________________.

8. REAL-LIFE INTEGRATION

Spiritual strength and endurance are revealed in repeated responses to difficult situations in:

- how you continue when motivation declines.
- whether you're consistent when results are not visible.

- how you respond when pressure increases.
- whether you maintain direction without backing down.

Endurance is not passive survival. It is an active, consistent, and steady response. It shows up when a situation lasts longer than expected or a decision becomes difficult to maintain. It can be particularly obvious when tension increases and easier alternatives are available.

If you do not pray for perseverance, inconsistency will continue. Your prayer habits shape your endurance patterns. If you consistently pray for relief, you will weaken under pressure. But if you pray for strength, you will learn to remain steady during the trial.

Endurance is not built in moments,
but in habits, attitudes, and patterns.

9. TAKE THIS STEP TODAY

For the next seven days:

- Identify one area in which you have reduced effort due to difficulty.
- Write the original commitment in one clear sentence.
- Return to that exact level of effort without adjustment.
- Repeat this same action daily to restore consistency.

10. FINAL DECLARATION

I will rely on God's strength to endure every trial.

Chapter 32
VICTORY OVER TEMPTATION

Prayers of Eternal Significance – Spiritual Awareness

1. REFRAME THE PRIORITY

People pray for protection from trials, but seldom ask for victory over temptation. Yet Scripture places this at the center of our spiritual life. Jesus taught His followers to pray "Lead us not into temptation, but deliver us from evil." This is an ongoing necessity just like our "daily bread." When ignored, temptations quietly shape decisions and ultimately our focus and direction.

Our prayer life must recognize that the greatest threats are not always external pressures, but can be the result of internal weaknesses. This is not about eliminating the sources of sin. This is about what you do when you are tempted. Temptation cannot be completely eliminated. It must be continually faced and overcome.

2. WHAT THIS LOOKS LIKE

Victory over temptation is not about achieving sinless perfection, but about consistent resistance and dependence on God. It means:

- Recognizing temptation before rather than after your failure.
- Actively choosing obedience in specific moments.
- Depending on God's strength rather than your personal willpower.

It also means understanding that temptation is not random. It occurs in familiar places and situations like habits or thoughts that repeatedly lead in the same direction. Victory is maintained through intentional dependence on God.

3. EXPOSE THE GAP

Believers want to resist temptation, but they approach it inconsistently. They will:

- Fight temptation after it has already taken hold.
- Rely on personal resolve rather than prayer.
- Excuse small compromises.
- Repeat the same patterns without addressing the fundamental problem.

Their prayer is reactive and after failure they pray "Forgive me" or during high pressure situations pray "Help me." But the true need is to be more proactive:

- "Prepare me for what I will face today."
- "Strengthen me before I am tested."

The problem is you are unprepared. You can sincerely desire change while still repeatedly returning to the same struggle. Why? Your prayer approach has not changed your behavior. Without intentional prayer, temptation is allowed to resurface again and again.

You are not losing the battle in the moment.
You are entering it unprepared.

4. HOW TO PRAY DIFFERENTLY

When it comes to sin, evil, wickedness, and immorality your prayers are often incomplete. You pray for:

- Forgiveness after failure.
- Relief from consequences.
- Strength in general terms.

These are necessary, but totally insufficient. You rarely pray:

- "Show me where I am most vulnerable."
- "Interrupt this pattern before it begins."

- "Give me clarity in the moment of decision."
- "Strengthen my desire to obey, not just resist."
- "Warn me when I am nearing danger."

When the pattern continues, awareness comes too late, resistance is weak, and dependence on God is minimal. Your prayers must shift. Reset your prayer from reactive prayer to consistent and intentional preparation. You must always be ready to face temptation!

Victory over temptation is developed by praying earlier, more specifically, and more honestly. If you only respond after the enticement is real, you will be unprepared for the fight.

Stop underestimating temptation and start actively resisting it through God's power and intentional prayer.

5. TRANSFORMATIONAL PRAYER

Father, You know the areas in which I am most vulnerable. I confess that I often rely on my own strength and only turn to You after I have already struggled or failed.

Give me clarity and wisdom to recognize the allurement of sin early. Strengthen my desire to obey You, even when it is difficult or inconvenient.

Prepare me before I am tested. Guard my thoughts, improve my choices, and help me make the right decisions. When I feel the pull toward sin, remind me of what is true and give me the strength to choose what is right.

Teach me to depend on You daily. Lead me away from temptation and into a life of consistent and continual obedience.

6. SHORT ADDITIONAL PRAYERS

Strengthen Me Before I Am Tested
Lord, give me clarity *before* I am overcome by temptation.

Help Me Recognize Temptation Early
Father, make me aware of danger when I am most vulnerable.

Give Me the Strength to Choose Obedience
Lord, strengthen my desire to do what is right.

Guard My Thoughts and Actions
Father, control my reactions so I can overcome temptation.

7. PERSONAL DIAGNOSTIC

1. Where do I face the same temptations repeatedly?
2. Do I pray before I am tested, or only after I struggle?
3. What situations make me the most vulnerable?
4. Do I minimize behaviors that need to be addressed?
5. What am I tolerating that I know needs to change?

Your answers expose where temptation you have underestimated has been allowed to impact your life. When poor habits remain unchallenged, vulnerability increases and resistance weakens. This reveals a pattern of reacting after failure rather than preparing before it occurs.

What is tolerated will continue and what is not addressed will return. Minimizing behavior does not reduce its impact; it allows it to remain active. What you do not resist will continue. If this is not addressed, the pattern will repeat.

Identify the pattern you have allowed to continue and bring it into clear focus. Decide what you will confront and act on it without delay.

My response:

I will ______________________________.

8. REAL-LIFE INTEGRATION

Victory over temptation is shaped in ordinary moments:

- In how you respond to frustration.
- In what you allow your mind to dwell on.
- In decisions made when no one is watching.
- In habits that form quietly in the background.

Sin rarely appears suddenly. It builds up through repeated exposure and unguarded moments. What you prepare for in prayer will shape how you respond in these moments and in times when you are under pressure.

What you allow consistently
will shape who you become.

9. TAKE THIS STEP TODAY

Identify one recurring area of temptation in your life. Each morning this week, pray specifically about that one area:

- Name it clearly.
- Ask for awareness.
- Ask for strength in the moment of decision.
- Keep the focus narrow and consistent.

10. FINAL DECLARATION

I will resist temptation and stand firm relying on God's power.

Chapter 33
REJOICING IN GOD

Prayers of Eternal Significance – Joy and Satisfaction

1. REFRAME THE PRIORITY

Most people pursue joy in order to live life under better circumstances. Few pursue joy as a response grounded in the nature of God Himself. When joy is anchored in God, it becomes durable and independent of changing conditions.

Joy matters eternally because what you delight in shapes what you think and pursue. If your satisfaction is rooted in worldly outcomes, your life will be determined by them. If your satisfaction rests in God, your life will align with the nature of God and what has value.

2. WHAT THIS LOOKS LIKE

Rejoicing in God is the intentional choice to find satisfaction, delight, and contentment in who God is and what He offers. It is independent of immediate and temporary worldly circumstances. It includes:

- Valuing God above changing circumstances.
- Choosing gratitude when conditions are not ideal.
- Recognizing His character as a source of stability.
- Maintaining perspective when emotions fluctuate.
- Refusing to let disappointment define your outlook.
- Returning focus to what is eternal rather than what is shifting and temporary.

Joy is not automatic. Like gratitude, it is both a decision and a practiced attitude.

3. EXPOSE THE GAP

If you are struggling with contentment, you may be looking for it in the wrong places. The gap appears in subtle ways:

- We feel steady only when things go well.
- We lose perspective when outcomes change.
- We become discouraged when progress is slow.
- We depend on external conditions to feel stable.

These difficulties occur because you are depending on the wrong source for your joy. You cannot expect circumstances to supply what only God can provide. External values do not produce lasting stability. If outcomes change or shift so will your sense of peace and satisfaction.

If you depend on the world to supply your joy, you will ultimately be disappointed. When your focus is on what is happening around you, your joy will be fragile.

4. HOW TO PRAY DIFFERENTLY

When joy is unstable, prayer often focuses on changing conditions. You may pray:

- "Fix this situation."
- "Make things better."
- "Change these circumstances."
- "Remove what is difficult."

It is far more effective to pray:

- "Re-center my satisfaction in You."
- "Teach me to remain steady regardless of outcomes."
- "Correct me when I depend on circumstances for stability."
- "Strengthen my ability to find joy in who You are."

You may be hoping your prayer improves conditions while leaving your dependence misplaced and untouched. This is where your prayer must shift from outcome-based joy to God-centered joy. Stop praying "make things better so I feel steady" and instead pray "make me steady regardless of what changes."

Joy is not sustained by outcomes. It is sustained by alignment with God and His laws. Joy grows when God becomes the focus, not the outcome. If your joy depends on outcomes, it will remain unstable.

Stop looking for joy in circumstances and start finding your joy in God.

5. TRANSFORMATIONAL PRAYER

Father, I confess that I often look to circumstances to provide what only You can sustain. When things go well, I feel steady. When they do not, I lose perspective and become unsettled.

Expose patterns where I depend on results, progress, or comfort instead of You. Do not allow me to continue trying to build stability on what is temporary.

Teach me to find joy in who You are, not just in what You do. Re-center my thinking so that my satisfaction is grounded in what does not change.

Strengthen my ability to remain steadfast regardless of the circumstances. Establish in me a steady, enduring joy that remains anchored in You.

6. SHORT ADDITIONAL PRAYERS

Center My Joy
Lord, anchor my satisfaction in You.

Stability in Uncertainty
Father, keep me steady when circumstances change.

Correct My Focus
Lord, help me return to what is constant and eternal.

Enduring Joy
Father, build a joy in me that is not dependent on outcomes.

7. PERSONAL DIAGNOSTIC

1. When circumstances change, does my sense of stability change with them?
2. What do I depend on most to feel satisfied?
3. Where has disappointment reshaped my outlook?
4. Do I focus on improved conditions?
5. What am I relying on that I cannot maintain?

Your answers will indicate what your stability depends on. When satisfaction is tied to circumstances, your outlook shifts with every new result and steadiness is lost. This demonstrates you are relying on what cannot consistently sustain you.

What you depend on determines how you respond when conditions shift. If your source is unstable, your perspective will be as well. Identify what you are relying on for satisfaction and correct that focus, if necessary. Decide what you will rely on and align your focus accordingly.

My response:

I will ______________________________.

8. REAL-LIFE INTEGRATION

Rejoicing in God is revealed in daily responses:

- How you react when expectations are not met or circumstances are difficult.
- If your perspective remains steady under pressure.

- How you interpret delays, setbacks, uncertainty, or disappointment.
- If your satisfaction depends on worldly result, or alignment with God.

These are not isolated situations. If you do not pray specifically, instability will surely continue. Your prayer habits shape your emotional patterns. If you consistently pray for better circumstances, your stability will depend on them. If you pray for realignment and relationship with God, your stability will begin to anchor in what matters most.

Joy will follow what you prioritize.

9. TAKE THIS STEP TODAY

For the next seven days:

- Identify one situation that is affecting your outlook.
- Write one sentence about who God is in that situation.
- Read that sentence each morning and evening.
- Refuse to adjust it based on changing conditions.

10. FINAL DECLARATION

I will find my joy and satisfaction in God alone.

Chapter 34
LIVING A FRUITFUL LIFE

Prayers of Eternal Significance – Eternal Impact

1. REFRAME THE PRIORITY

Everyone wants a productive life. Few aim for a fruitful one. Productivity measures activity but fruitfulness measures what remains after you are gone. You can accomplish much and still produce very little that endures. Having a full schedule and many friends is not the same as a meaningful life.

This matters because what is visible now is not what ultimately remains. Fruit is defined by what lasts beyond the immediate timeframe. A fruitful life is not measured by what you complete, but by what continues because you lived.

2. WHAT THIS LOOKS LIKE

Living a fruitful life is the intentional pursuit of actions and priorities that produce an enduring impact rather than a temporary result. It includes:

- Focusing on what has long-term value rather than immediate payoff.
- Investing in people, character, and truth rather than worldly values.
- Choosing depth over volume in key areas.
- Acting with purpose rather than reacting to pressure.
- Aligning daily effort with what ultimately matters.
- Measuring success by lasting influence rather than visible result.

A fruitful life is not about the volume of what is produced. It is about producing what endures and is revealed over time.

3. EXPOSE THE GAP

You do not necessarily reject fruitfulness, but you find it easy to become distracted or misdirected in your daily lifestyle. This gap often appears in subtle ways:

- We fill our time with what seems timely or urgent rather than what is eternally important.
- We measure success by completion instead of impact.
- We stay busy but rarely evaluate the value of what we are doing or have produced.
- We prioritize visible temporary results over meaningful long-term eternal investments.

Thus, you are not unproductive. You are misaligned. The underlying problem is you assume that activity leads to some valuable impact. But valuable activity does not necessarily produce meaningful impact. This creates a life that can feel full but produces little that endures.

Fruitful living is not lost in a moment. It is crowded out by unexamined activity, busyness, and unimportant things.

When everything feels necessary,
nothing is chosen carefully.

4. HOW TO PRAY DIFFERENTLY

When fruitfulness is low, it is often the result of prayer focused on outcomes and visible success. You pray "Bless what I am doing" or "Make this successful." You may even say "Help me accomplish more."

These are understandable, but are not on target. Pray:

- "Show me what truly produces lasting impact."
- "Remove what fills my time but produces little."
- "Redirect my focus toward what endures."
- "Make my life effective, not just active."

Your prayer should not ask for better results while ignoring whether the effort itself is aligned with the plans of God. Stop praying "help me do more" and pray "help me do what lasts."

Fruitful living is not the result of increased effort. It is the result of aligned and meaningful effort. A fruitful life is the result of consistent aligned prayer. If you pursue activity without alignment, you will remain busy but not fruitful.

Stop measuring success by temporary results and start pursuing fruit that lasts eternally.

5. TRANSFORMATIONAL PRAYER

Father, I confess that I often measure my life by what I complete rather than by what truly lasts. I fill my time with activity, but I do not always consider whether my effort produces a lasting impact.

Show me where I am investing in what is temporary and expose patterns of busyness that crowd out what truly matters. Do not allow me to continue spending energy on what produces little that endures.

Redirect my focus toward what has lasting value. Help me choose wisely where I invest my time, energy, and attention. Establish in me a pattern of living that produces fruit that remains. I surrender my desire to measure success by activity.

6. SHORT ADDITIONAL PRAYERS

Focus on What Lasts
Lord, direct my attention toward what has lasting value.

Remove Distraction
Father, clear away what fills my time but produces little.

Align My Effort
Lord, help me invest my energy where it truly matters.

Lasting Impact
Father, allow me to produce fruit that endures.

7. PERSONAL DIAGNOSTIC

1. What is filling most of my time? Does it produce lasting impact?
2. Where am I busy but not truly effective?
3. What important area am I neglecting because of other constant activity?
4. Do I measure success by completion or lasting impact?
5. What am I doing that is not producing much but feels necessary?

Your answers reveal where your time and effort are being directed. When activity replaces effectiveness, busyness fills space without producing lasting impact. This produces a consistent ongoing cycle in which busyness is mistaken for significance. What truly matters is neglected.

What you do determines what your life produces. Productivity without purpose leads to limited results. What you pursue determines what remains. Identify efforts that are not producing lasting impact and decide what you will focus on and act on with intention.

My response:

I will ______________________________.

8. REAL-LIFE INTEGRATION

Fruitfulness is revealed in your daily priorities:

- In what you choose to deserve your attention.
- In how you respond to demands for your attention.
- In whether you evaluate the impact of your actions.

- In how you decide what deserves your best effort of time, energy, and focus.
- In whether your efforts create ongoing impact or just temporary outcomes.

These are not occasional situations. They are repeated patterns that may be required daily. When you do not pray in alignment with eternal values, misalignment continues.

Your prayer habits shape your priorities. If you consistently pray for success in what you are doing, you will reinforce these patterns, both good and bad. If you pray for alignment, your priorities will begin to change.

A fruitful life is built through intentional selection of priorities.

9. TAKE THIS STEP TODAY

For the next seven days:

- Identify one activity that consumes time but produces little lasting impact.
- Reduce or eliminate it for the week.
- Replace that time with one intentional action that contributes to eternal results.

Do not expand beyond one change. Keep the focus deliberate and controlled.

10. FINAL DECLARATION

I will pursue a life that produces lasting eternal fruit.

When we pray, we align ourselves with the purposes of God and tap into the power of the Almighty

David Jeremiah

FINAL REFLECTION

Resetting your prayers. Redirecting your life.

This book has not asked you to pray more. It has asked you to pray differently. If you never question the content of your prayers, you will repeat what feels natural, urgent, or familiar.

Over time, those patterns settle in. You assume that because you are praying, you are praying rightly. But prayer can be consistent and still be misdirected. It can be sincere and still be incomplete. A life of prayer is not measured by frequency alone, but by alignment with what matters most.

This often requires a *reset.*

We have considered four major areas: God, others, the world, and your own life. That order is intentional. When prayer begins with God, it recalibrates everything else. When it includes others, it breaks self-centered patterns. When it extends to the world, it connects you to eternal purpose. When it returns to your own life, it does so with clarity and direction that was absent before.

If you are honest, you have probably seen patterns that need correction. Your prayers may have centered on personal needs more than God's purposes. You may have been asking for outcomes without asking for transformation. You may have avoided certain prayers altogether: those that required surrender, change, or obedience.

What you do next matters more than what you have just studied or read. Do not try to change everything at once. That will not work. Choose one area where the gap is clear and act on it. Establish one new pattern of prayer that reflects what you want to accomplish. Then let that pattern begin to shape your future thinking, decisions, and responses before moving on to the next area.

As your prayers change, your engagement will begin to shift. You will ask different questions. You will become less concerned with immediate relief and more focused on lasting impact. You will respond with greater steadiness because prayers of eternal significance reshape the one who is praying.

God is not waiting for perfect words. He is inviting committed hearts to align with His plans. The goal is a life brought into agreement with what matters to Him.

This kind of prayer produces clarity without anxiety, conviction without harshness, and steadiness without passivity. You begin to live from a different perspective. Decisions become less reactive and relationships become more intentional.

Even your struggles will be approached differently. You are no longer asking "How do I get through this" but "What is God doing and how should I respond faithfully?"

Your prayers reveal what you believe matters most. They quietly train your life to move in that direction.

Changing your prayers is not a small adjustment. It is a decisive shift. Return to these pages when needed and let them correct you, not just inform you. Resist the drift back to old patterns. Stay aware of what you are asking, and why you are asking it.

Pray in a way that aligns your life with eternity.

Pray with alignment and purpose.

Finish with an impact!

Free PDF

Life Improvement Principles

You can live your best life!

Welcome to a journey of discovery! In case you have forgotten, your actions have consequences. Unlock your potential! This book (60+ pages) provides the overview of all our strategies and wisdom principles to live your best life. You *can* transform your life! Get your wisdom-based roadmap to a better life and unlock the possibilities for growth and success.

FREE PDF

https://getwisdompublishing.com/resource-registration/

Kindle ebook for 99 cents:

https://www.amazon.com/dp/B0FG883KZM

Ebook

Free PDF

Make it your life goal to be the best you can be!

Discover Wisdom and live the life you deserve.

The Wisdom Prayer Series

Personal Daily Prayer Guide

Prayer Resource and Journal

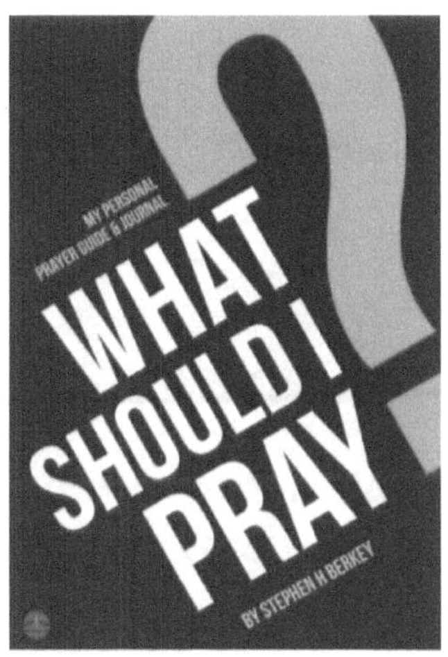

Know what to pray.
Pray based on Bible verses.
Strengthen your prayer life.
Access reference resources.
Pray with eternal implications.
Write your own prayers if desired.
Organize and focus your prayer time.
Learn what the Bible says about prayer.
Find encouragement and advice on how to pray.
Reduce frustration and distraction in your prayer time.

Get your copy today!

https://www.amazon.com/dp/1952359260/

The Wisdom Prayer Series

Prayer Can Change Your Life!

Biblical Prayers That
Transform the Christian Life

- Know God more deeply
- Trust God completely
- Seek God's wisdom for life's decisions
- Renew your mind through God's truth
- Grow in Christ-like character
- Live a holy life
- Love others as Christ loves
- Find strength in trials
- Live with eternal perspective
- Finish the race of faith faithfully

These prayers move beyond temporary needs and focus on the spiritual foundations that shape a life devoted to God.

Let These Prayers Shape Your Walk With God.

https://www.amazon.com/dp/1952359813

The Wisdom Prayer Series

Are You Walking With Jesus?

Devotional

Are You Walking With Jesus is designed to support a steady and thoughtful rhythm of discipleship rather than a hurried reading plan. The goal is to allow prayer, Scripture, and reflection to shape your devotional life for 60 days.

This devotional invites you to consider a simple but life-shaping question: *Are you walking with Jesus?* Over the next sixty days, these prayers and reflections are designed to help you deepen your relationship with Christ, align your heart with His will, and live each day in faithful discipleship.

https://www.amazon.com/dp/1952359791

About the Author

After 25 years as an actuary, and 20 years as an entrepreneur, Steve began his third career as an author in 2020, when he published The OBSCURE Bible Study Series and in 2024 began publishing the Jesus Follower Bible Study Series. This book is now the fourth book in the Wisdom Prayer Series. He is a member of The Church at Station Hill in Spring Hill, TN, a regional campus of Brentwood Baptist Church, Brentwood. TN.

www.getwisdompublishing.com

Contact Information & Links

The Wisdom Prayer Series

https://www.amazon.com/dp/B0GX31YV7f

Personal Daily Prayer Guide

https://www.amazon.com/What-Should-Pray-Personal-Journal/dp/1952359260/

Can Prayer Change Your Life?

https://www.amazon.com/dp/1952359813

Are You Walking with Jesus

https://www.amazon.com/dp/1952359791

The *OBSCURE* Bible Study Series

https://www.amazon.com/dp/B08T7TL1B1

The Jesus Follower Bible Study Series

https://www.amazon.com/dp/B0DHP39P5J

Get Wisdom – General Information

www.getwisdompublishing.com

NOTE: You Can Help!

Please leave an honest review on the Amazon Sales Page
https://www.amazon.com/dp/195235983X

Thanks so much

GETWISDOM
PUBLISHING

www.ingramcontent.com/pod-product-compliance
Lightning Source LLC
LaVergne TN
LVHW041928090826
845145LV00017B/2293

* 9 7 8 1 9 5 2 3 5 9 8 3 5 *